Crime and Punishment in America

in America

BIOGRAPHIES

Crime and Punishment in America

BIOGRAPHIES

Richard C. Hanes and Kelly Rudd
Sarah Hermsen, Project Editor

U·X·L
An imprint of Thomson Gale,
a part of The Thomson Corporation

THOMSON
GALE

Detroit • New York • San Francisco • San Diego • New Haven, Conn. • Waterville, Maine • London • Munich

THOMSON
★
™
GALE

Crime and Punishment in America: Biographies
Richard C. Hanes and Kelly Rudd

Project Editor
Sarah Hermsen

Rights Acquisitions and Management
Ann Taylor

Imaging and Multimedia
Leitha Etheridge-Sims, Lezlie Light, Dan Newell

Product Design
Michelle Dimercurio

Composition
Evi Seoud

Manufacturing
Rita Wimberley

Library of Congress Cataloging-in-Publication Data
Hanes, Richard Clay, 1946–
    Crime and punishment in America. Biographies / Richard C. Hanes and Kelly Rudd ; Sarah Hermsen, project editor.
        p. cm. — (Crime and punishment in America reference library)
    Includes bibliographical references and index.
    ISBN 0-7876-9167-4 (hardcover : alk. paper)
    1. Criminals—United States—Biography.   2. Criminal justice personnel—United States—Biography.   3. Criminologists—United States Biography.   I. Rudd, Kelly, 1954–   II. Hermsen, Sarah.   III. Title.   IV. Series.
    HV6785.H34 2005
    364.973′092′2—dc22   2004017066

Printed in the United States of America
10 9 8 7 6 5 4 3

Contents

Reader's Guide

Crimes are forbidden acts considered harmful or dangerous. They fall outside society's rules of proper behavior. Some acts—such as murder, robbery, and rape—violate the behavioral codes of almost every society. Other acts may be considered crimes in one culture but not in another. In criminal law both society and the individual victim, when there is one, are considered harmed by crimes. Each crime threatens some aspect of society; for example, white-collar crime—business-related crimes such as fraud or embezzlement—threatens the economy, and the illegal dumping of waste threatens the quality of the environment. For this reason, a victim's approval is not necessary for the government to prosecute a crime and punish the offender.

Over the past four centuries, crime and punishment in America have steadily changed as society has changed. Some types of behavior considered criminal in colonial times, such as idleness and heresy, have ceased to be treated as crimes, while other behaviors, such as computer hacking and toxic-waste dumping, have since been added to the list of prohibited acts. Technological advances have improved the abilities of criminals to commit crimes and avoid detection, but such advances have also aided law enforcement officials in their work. The rise of the automobile in the early twentieth century resulted in an increase in interstate crime and faster getaways for the criminals, but with their new patrol cars police were able to respond more readily to calls for help. At the end of the twentieth century, advances in telecommunications introduced new methods of breaking the law but also gave law enforcement officials many new ways to catch criminals and expanded crime-fighting to an international stage.

In a democratic society, the rules of behavior that maintain social order come from citizens, not from a church or from a royal head of state such as a king. These rules are set through judicial decisions, legal history, and cultural tradition. Rules are also established by legislatures, or law-making bodies, acting through democratic principles by passing laws of government based on the beliefs, opinions, and desires of the citizens. The rules and consequent punishments for violations are organized in sets and written down. Those who break the codes of criminal law in the United States are subject to the U.S. criminal justice system—arrest by law enforcement authorities, court trial, and punishment.

As English colonists established settlements in the New World beginning in the early seventeenth century, they brought English common law with them. This law included the well-known process of accusation, arrest, decision to prosecute or to dismiss, trial, judgment, and punishment. However, in colonial America rigid social order had to be maintained for survival of the first settlements and the colonists had to modify the English legal system to accommodate their unique situation in the New World. For example, there were often too few people residing in a given area for jury trials to be practical. In addition, many areas lacked a person with the proper law training to serve as a judge. Often an officer of the colony or a respected member of the community made legal decisions. Another difference between English courts and the developing American legal system involved the death penalty—the punishment of death to those convicted of serious crimes. American criminal courts applied the death penalty to fewer crimes than English courts. Colonists were also more respectful of individual civil liberties, believing the accused had a legal right to fairness.

With independence from England following the American Revolution (1775–83), a new American criminal justice system came into being. The common-law crime system gradually gave way to statutory criminal law. In contrast to common law, in statutory law acts are deemed criminal when the legislative body responds to a changing society's needs and passes a law prohibiting some activity or behavior. During the nineteenth century other basic changes in criminal justice arrived, such as professional policing and penitentiaries, or prisons.

Although fairness in the criminal justice system is a trait traditionally valued by American citizens, it has not always been evident. Throughout much of American history political power was held by one segment of society—white Protestant males. As a result black Americans, immigrant minorities, women, and other segments of society felt the full weight of law for much of American history. For example in the early twentieth century women could be arrested for voting and blacks could be convicted and executed simply because they were accused of a crime, regardless of the evidence available. The march for equality before the law and fairness in criminal justice procedures as guaranteed by the U.S. Constitution made steady progress through the late twentieth century.

The criminal justice system today is composed of many parts and numerous players. Legislatures, usually under pressure from society, make laws defining crime. Police and detectives apprehend offenders. Courts, prosecutors, defense lawyers, and judges determine the offenders' guilt. Prison wardens and guards, probation officers, and parole board members carry out the sentences. Criminal justice can be found in many varied settings, ranging from street community policing on bicycles to high-tech forensic laboratories; from isolation cells in a maximum-security prison to the historic chamber of the U.S. Supreme Court.

For an action to be considered a crime, not only does a loss or injury have to occur, but there must typically be a proven willful "intent" to commit the act. A harmful action that is an accident and did not occur from irresponsible behavior is not usually considered a crime. Crimes defined in the codes of law are either felonies or misdemeanors. Felonies are major crimes resulting in prison sentences of longer than one year. For certain felonies, namely murder cases, and in certain states, the punishment might be the death penalty, also known as capital punishment. Other felonies include robbery and rape. Misdemeanors are minor crimes punishable by fines or short periods of time, up to one year, in a local jail. Misdemeanors are sometimes called "petty" crimes, including such acts of petty theft as stealing a lawnmower from a shed or a compact disc player from a car.

Academics search for reasons why social deviance grew during the twentieth century. Criminologists and other professionals attempted to find the causes of crime in the hope of finding a cure for crime. Even though crime can be highly predictable—despite a seeming randomness at times—progress has been slow in isolating the causes.

Even less clear than the root cause of crime is the effect of the justice system on criminal activity. Crime seems to increase even as efforts to combat crime are intensified. Crime impacts millions of people, and the prevention, control, prosecution, rehabilitation, and punishment of criminals result in extraordinary expenses—not to mention the losses resulting from the crimes themselves. By the end of the twentieth century, operation of the criminal justice system at federal, state, and local levels cost $130 billion a year in addition to the $20 billion a year in losses to crime. On the other hand, industries related to crime and punishment create thousands of jobs, and the various forms of crime-related entertainment bring in many millions of dollars.

Features

Crime and Punishment in America: Biographies presents the life stories of twenty-six individuals who have played key roles in the history of crime and punishment. People from all walks of life are included. Some held prominent national roles in developing or influencing the U.S. criminal justice system; others were defendants in key court trials that contributed significantly to the field. Profiled are well-known figures such as former Federal Bureau of Investigation (FBI) director J. Edgar Hoover, authors Charles Dickens and Truman Capote, Supreme Court justice Felix Frankfurter, domestic terrorists Ted Kaczynski and Timothy McVeigh, U.S. senator Estes Kefauver, defense attorney Clarence Darrow, and social reformer Jane Addams. A number of lesser-known individuals are included as well, such as early female lawyers Belva Ann Lockwood and Arabella Mansfield, criminal defendants Daniel McNaughtan and Ernest Miranda, New York City police chief George Washington Walling, and political radical Emma Goldman. Each chapter contains sidebars highlighting people and events of special interest as well as a list of additional sources students can go to for more information. More than fifty black-and-white photographs illustrate the text. The volume begins with a timeline of important events in the history of space exploration and a "Words to Know" section that introduces students to difficult or unfamiliar terms. The volume concludes with a general bibliography and a subject index so students can easily find the people, places, and events discussed throughout *Crime and Punishment in America: Biographies*.

Crime and Punishment in America Reference Library

Crime and Punishment in America: Biographies is only one component of the three-part Crime and Punishment in America Reference Library. The set includes two other titles:

Crime and Punishment in America: Almanac (two volumes) presents a comprehensive overview of the development of the American justice system. The two-volume set covers in twenty-five chapters various topics including violent crime, crimes against property, cyber crime, terrorism, environmental crime, organized crime, public order crime, school violence, and white-collar crime, from the first European settlements of the seventeenth century to the early twenty-first century. The *Almanac* also describes elements of the criminal justice system including courts, policing, forensic science, corrections, military justice, American Indian criminal justice systems, and juvenile justice. Additional chapters address the influences of moral and religious values as well as the media on crime and punishment.

Crime and Punishment in America: Primary Sources (one volume) tells the story of the criminal justice system in the words of the people who shaped the field and the laws that contributed to its development. Eighteen excerpted documents touch on a wide range of topics related to crime and punishment. Included are excerpts from colonial and federal laws, such as the Harrison Narcotic Drug Act of 1914; the Magna Carta; trial transcripts; newspaper accounts; government documents; various publications, including "The Al Qaeda Training Manual" and Charles Dickens's *American Notes;* and notable speeches.

A cumulative index of all three titles in the Crime and Punishment in America Reference Library is also available.

Comments and Suggestions

We welcome your comments on *Crime and Punishment in America* and suggestions for other topics to consider. Please write to: Editor, *Crime and Punishment in America: Biographies,* U•X•L, 27500 Drake Road, Farmington Hills, Michigan 48331-3535; call toll-free: 1-800-877-4253; fax to 248-699-8097; or send e-mail via http://www.gale.com.

Timeline of Events

1215 King John signs the Magna Carta in England, recognizing certain fundamental liberties and rights of landowners.

1609 English and other European colonists begin settling the East Coast of North America, adapting the English common-law criminal justice system to the New World. One such adaptation is establishing the position of sheriff.

1611 The colony of Virginia issues "Lawes Divine, Morall and Martiall" to maintain a strict control over the settlement's residents during its infancy.

1740s Slave patrols are established in the southern colonies to monitor slave activities. Such patrols are considered a forerunner of policing.

1775 The American Revolution (1775–83) erupts, driven partly by the colonists' desire to increase fairness and obtain legal protections in the criminal justice system.

1787 The U.S. Constitution is adopted, establishing a new national governmental system that includes a

Supreme Court and gives Congress authority to establish other federal courts as needed.

1787　The first prison reform organization is established in Philadelphia, the Philadelphia Society for Alleviating the Miseries of Public Prisons, promoting rehabilitation over punishment.

1790　Philadelphia opens the Walnut Street Jail, introducing a four-tier prisoner system based on type of offender. The system includes isolation for some prisoners.

1791　The first ten amendments to the U.S. Constitution, known collectively as the Bill of Rights, are adopted. The amendments contain several sections concerning crime and punishment, including freedom from unreasonable search and seizure, freedom from self-incrimination, the right to legal counsel, and freedom from cruel and unusual punishment.

1829　Pennsylvania opens the Eastern State Penitentiary, also known as Cherry Hill, which becomes the model for the Separate System, in which inmates are placed in solitary confinement around the clock.

1831　**Gustave de Beaumont**, a French statesman commissioned by the King of France to inspect American prison systems, journeys with his friend and noted historian Alexis de Tocqueville, spending several months examining American prisons.

1835　New York becomes the first state to stop public executions.

1842　World-famous British novelist **Charles Dickens**, who held a personal interest in criminal law and prison reform, tours America, visiting several modern American prisons including Cherry Hill, an international showplace for prisoner isolation. Dickens called the prison intolerably cruel in his *American Notes,* published later that year.

1843　**Daniel McNaughtan**, tried for the murder of a British government official, is found not guilty by reason of insanity. The case leads to a widely used legal precedent known as the McNaughtan Rules, used to determine a person's criminal responsibility.

1844 New York City establishes the first city police force to address the rising crime rate.

1846 Michigan becomes the first state to abolish the death penalty.

1850 **Allan Pinkerton** leaves the Chicago police force to organize his own agency, the Pinkerton National Detective Agency. He pioneers several practices, including the use of wanted posters featuring the criminals he was seeking.

1861 With the outbreak of the American Civil War, Allan Pinkerton is appointed head of the first Secret Service in America. Using the false name Major E. J. Allen, Pinkerton provides information to Washington from behind enemy lines in the South as well as detecting treasonable counterespionage activities in the North.

1866 **Belva Ann Lockwood** moves to Washington, D.C., and campaigns for the National Woman Suffrage Association, an organization seeking voting rights for women. The following year she helps found the Universal Franchise Association, Washington's first suffrage group.

1869 After studying law on her own, **Arabella Mansfield** becomes the first woman admitted to a state bar to practice law in the United States. She earns a formal law degree three years later.

1871 Belva Ann Lockwood is admitted to the newly founded National University Law School of Washington and completes her degree requirements in 1873. She is admitted to the District of Columbia bar and then to the District's Supreme Court.

January 24, 1873 Susan B. Anthony is indicted for illegally voting in Rochester, New York, the November prior. She enters a not guilty plea. Anthony is found guilty of violating the law banning women from voting; for her punishment she must pay a fine.

July 1874 **George Washington Walling** begins his tenure as Police Chief of New York City and serves until June 1885. Due to Walling's work, professionalism in policing makes giant strides across the nation in the latter half of the nineteenth century.

March 1879 Belva Ann Lockwood becomes the first woman admitted to practice before the U.S. Supreme Court and the U.S. Court of Claims. She becomes the first woman to practice in the federal courts.

1889 **Jane Addams** rents a formerly elegant old house on Halsted Street in Chicago called Hull House and turns it into a settlement house, providing social services to a large immigrant community in the surrounding tenements.

1889 **Emma Goldman** joins the anarchist movement and participates in radical political activities in New York City. She was greatly influenced by events leading to the 1886 Haymarket trials in Chicago, Illinois, wherein an anarchist rally resulted in the bombing deaths of seven policemen. Four anarchist labor leaders were convicted of conspiracy and executed, though the actual bomber was never identified.

June 1893 **Lizzie Borden** is found not guilty of the December 1892 murder of her father and stepmother. The trial was a media sensation at the New Bedford Court House in Massachusetts.

August 1893 Emma Goldman is arrested for inciting a riot after addressing a public rally of some three thousand people at Union Square in New York City.

1894 **Clarence Darrow** defends Eugene V. Debs, a labor leader charged with crimes related to a strike against the Pullman Company. The trial marks the beginning of a series of criminal cases in which Darrow defends organized labor.

1899 Illinois becomes the first state to establish a separate court system for juveniles under pressure from Jane Addams and others in Chicago concerned with the growing numbers of immigrant street youth in Chicago.

1903 Emma Goldman, now dubbed "Red Emma," establishes the Free Speech League to promote the right to freedom of speech and freedom of assembly. She promotes other anarchists like Big Bill Haywood and his militant trade union.

1905   Pennsylvania creates the nation's first state police force.

1905   Bill Haywood and others form the radical labor organization the Industrial Workers of the World (IWW), known as "the Wobblies." The following year Haywood is charged with the murder of former Idaho governor, Frank R. Steunenberg. Defended by famous attorney Clarence Darrow, Haywood is acquitted in 1907 in the first trial to be covered by press wire services.

1908   The Bureau of Investigation is created in the U.S. Department of Justice to conduct investigations. It becomes the Federal Bureau of Investigation (FBI) in 1935.

1910   Congress passes the Mann Act, which prohibits taking women across state lines to engage in prostitution.

1912   Jane Addams becomes the first woman to make a nominating speech at a national political convention when she seconds the nomination of former president Theodore Roosevelt as the presidential candidate of the Progressive Party.

1917   **J. Edgar Hoover** is hired into the Alien Enemy Bureau of the U.S. Justice Department. He rises rapidly and is placed in charge of a unit in the Enemy Alien Registration Section. Hoover is responsible for gathering evidence on revolutionary and politically radical groups.

June 15, 1917   Emma Goldman, who has edited the monthly journal *Mother Earth* since 1906, is arrested on charges of conspiring to use her publication to convince people not to register for the military draft. She is deported to Russia along with hundreds of other anarchists.

1918   Bill Haywood and others are convicted under the Espionage Act for conspiring to interfere with the military draft for World War I. He is sentenced to twenty years in prison. While waiting for appeal, Haywood jumps bail and flees to the Soviet Union.

1919   J. Edgar Hoover is appointed chief of the new General Intelligence Division (GID) of the Bureau of Investigation.

1920 In response to the Red Scare—in which large numbers of people were being held by law authorities indefinitely because of their political beliefs—Jane Addams and defense attorney Felix Frankfurter are among those who establish the American Civil Liberties Union (ACLU) to protect the rights of individuals, including defendants in criminal trials.

August 26, 1920 The Nineteenth Amendment to the Constitution guaranteeing American women the right to vote is adopted.

1924 Clarence Darrow gives a dramatic plea against the death penalty to the court in the Chicago murder trial of Nathan Leopold and Richard Loeb. Darrow saved over one hundred accused murderers from execution.

May 1924 J. Edgar Hoover, at the age of twenty-nine, is named director of the Bureau of Investigation, a position he would hold until his death in May 1972 at the age of seventy-seven. In that role Hoover contributes to national stability and security during several periods of international and domestic crises and establishes a world-class crime-fighting organization.

July 1925 The Scopes case comes to trial with considerable national attention. Clarence Darrow defends a Tennessee schoolteacher charged with teaching evolution. One thousand people crowd the courthouse as hundreds of reporters cover the eight-day event, which is broadcast live over the radio to millions of homes and filmed for newsreels. The live radio broadcast from the courtroom was the first ever for a criminal trial.

1927 The first women's federal prison is established in West Virginia.

April 1927 In a trial followed internationally, two Italian immigrants, Nicola Sacco and Bartolomeo Vanzetti, are convicted of murder and robbery and sentenced to death in the small industrial town of South Braintree, Massachusetts. **Felix Frankfurter** and others challenge the lack of concrete evidence and unsuccessfully pressure the governor to reverse the conviction.

1929 President Herbert Hoover becomes the first U.S. president to identify crime as a key national issue in his inaugural address. Hoover appoints George Wicker-sham as head of the National Commission on Law Observance and Enforcement to examine all aspects of the U.S. criminal justice system. The commission issues fourteen reports by 1931.

1930s **Sally Stanford** sets up a business in the Tenderloin district of San Francisco. She employs professional prostitutes, creates an inviting atmosphere, and sees business flourish, attracting a wealthy clientele from the city.

1931 Jane Addams becomes the first American woman to receive the Nobel Peace Prize.

1931 **Thomas Dewey** leaves his Wall Street job to join the U.S. attorney's office for the southern district of New York. As a prosecutor during the 1930s, he aggressively prosecutes New York's most powerful organized crime figures, obtaining seventy-two convictions out of seventy-three prosecutions.

March 25, 1931 Nicknamed the **Scottsboro Boys,** Olen Montgomery, Clarence Norris, Haywood Patterson, Ozie Powell, Willie Roberson, Charles Weems, Eugene Williams, Andy Wright, and Roy Wright are arrested at Paint Rock, Alabama, for allegedly raping two white women on a freight train. For the next six years their case would change U.S. criminal law, resulting in two important Supreme Court decisions affecting criminal procedure.

1939 **Estes Kefauver** from Tennessee is elected to the U.S. House of Representatives, where he serves for nine years before being elected to the U.S. Senate. He remains a senator until his death in 1963.

1939 Criminologist Edwin Sutherland introduces the concept of white-collar crime.

January 30, 1939 Felix Frankfurter is sworn in as Associate Justice on the U.S. Supreme Court and serves on the high court for twenty-three years.

1941 The American Society of Criminology, originally called the National Association of College Police Officials, is founded.

1947 Edwin Sutherland publishes the landmark *Principles of Criminology*. Two years later he publishes *White-Collar Crime*.

1948 Republican Party candidate for president Thomas Dewey losses to Harry Truman in one of the greatest upsets in American political history. Dewey serves as governor of New York until 1955.

1950 Estes Kefauver chairs the Senate's Special Committee on Organized Crime in Interstate Commerce, more commonly known as the "Kefauver Committee," which exposes to the public for the first time a powerful underworld made up of mobsters and crooked politicians.

1961 The U.S. Supreme Court in its *Mapp v. Ohio* ruling establishes the criteria for preventing illegal searches and seizures.

March 13, 1963 Ernest Miranda is arrested in Phoenix, Arizona, as a suspect in the armed robbery of a bank worker. While in police custody, Miranda signed a written confession to the robbery, as well as the kidnap and rape of an eighteen-year-old woman in the desert outside Phoenix. The police interrogated Miranda for two hours without advising him he had the right to remain silent or to have an attorney present during questioning.

1966 Truman Capote creates a new type of true-crime literature, known as the nonfiction novel, with the publication of *In Cold Blood*. The book details the brutal murder of a Kansas family. It is produced as a popular Hollywood movie in 1967.

1966 Sally Stanford publishes her autobiography, *Lady of the House*, addressing vice crime in San Francisco.

June 13, 1966 The U.S. Supreme Court issues its landmark ruling in *Miranda v. Arizona*, confirming that for a confession to be admissible in a court of law it must be given voluntarily. The resulting Miranda rights guide police departments in the arrest and interrogation of suspects.

1967 Physician **Sam Sheppard** is acquitted for the murder of his wife in July 1954 in a trial that includes pioneering work in crime scene investigation and blood evidence. Sheppard was initially convicted and spent ten years in the Ohio Penitentiary. In 1966 the Supreme Court rules that Sheppard did not receive a fair trial due to media coverage. His story inspires a highly popular network television series and, later, a Hollywood movie, both known as *The Fugitive.*

1967   The president's Commission on Law Enforcement and Administration of Justice issues a report on organized crime and other aspects of the U.S. criminal justice system after a two-year study.

1972   The U.S. Supreme Court in *Furman v. Georgia* declares that the manner in which most states apply death penalty sentencing decisions violates the Constitution's protection from cruel and unusual punishment. In 1976, with *Gregg v. Georgia,* the Court upholds a new process for deciding on the death penalty using a separate sentencing trial.

1974   **Ted Bundy** begins his series of murders with the abduction and killing of nine young women taken from college campuses and recreation areas in the Pacific Northwest. These women are the first of twenty known victims.

1975   **Ivan Boesky** opens a business that specializes in trading stock in companies targeted by other companies for takeover.

1975   The National Organization for Victim Assistance (NOVA) is established to coordinate the victims' rights movement.

1976   Serial killer Ted Bundy is found guilty of kidnapping and sentenced to fifteen years in Utah State Prison. He escapes twice the following year, finally making his way to Florida.

1978   "Unabomber" **Ted Kaczynski** sends a packaged bomb to a professor at Northwestern University's Technological Institute in Evanston, Illinois, injuring a security guard who opens the suspicious package. This incident begins Kaczynski's series of terror bombings that last until the mid-1990s.

1979 In a sensational trial in Miami, Florida—the first televised nationally—serial killer Ted Bundy is convicted and sentenced to die in the electric chair.

1979 Dr. **Henry C. Lee**, a professor in forensic science at the University of New Haven, is appointed as the first chief criminalist for the State of Connecticut, a position he will hold until 2000.

1980 The victims' rights group Mothers against Drunk Driving (MADD) is formed to lobby Congress and states for tougher laws.

1982 Texas executes the first prisoner by lethal injection in the nation. Lethal injection becomes the primary method of execution in the United States.

1984 Congress passes the first law addressing computer-related crime, the Computer Fraud and Abuse Act, which prohibits interference with computer systems involved in interstate communications and economic trade.

November 14, 1986 Ivan Boesky pleads guilty to insider-trading charges, resulting in a $100 million fine and a three-year prison sentence. Boesky agrees to be a government informer to help break up other illegal activities on Wall Street.

1988 Robert Ressler co-authors *Sexual Homicide: Patterns and Motives,* which becomes the main resource criminal investigators use when they encounter a series of murders or sex crimes that appear to be linked. Ressler coins the term "serial killer" in developing the art of criminal profiling.

September 1988 The Securities and Exchange Commission (SEC) files charges against Michael Milken, accusing him of trading on inside information as well as filing false disclosure forms with the SEC in order to disguise stock ownership. In April 1990, Milken is sentenced to ten years in prison and fined $600 million.

January 24, 1989 With his legal appeals exhausted, serial killer Ted Bundy is electrocuted at the Florida State Prison in Starke.

1990 California passes the first law criminalizing stalking. Other states soon follow.

1992 The acquittal of Los Angeles police officers who had been videotaped beating black motorist Rodney King triggers extensive rioting for several days in the city, leaving some sixty people dead, twenty-three hundred injured, and six thousand arrested.

1994 In its "get tough on crime" push, Congress passes the Violent Crime Control and Law Enforcement Act, which increases the number of federal capital crimes from two to fifty-eight, provides $4 billion for new prison construction, adds 100,000 new police officers in police departments across the nation, and adopts "three strikes" sentencing guidelines for repeat offenders of federal crimes.

1994 Congress passes the Violence against Women Act, providing funding for assistance to women who are the victims of crime.

1995 After agreeing to a plea bargain in state court and being convicted on charges of operating a prostitution ring in Los Angeles in 1993, Heidi Fleiss is convicted in federal court of conspiracy, tax evasion, and money laundering.

1995 The murder trial of former football star O. J. Simpson is televised around the world, drawing attention to the U.S. criminal justice system, particularly forensic science.

September 19, 1995 *The Washington Post* and *The New York Times* publish the document "Industrial Society and Its Future," which becomes known as "The Unabomber Manifesto." It ultimately leads to the arrest of Ted Kaczynski, who pleads guilty to sixteen mail bombings on January 22, 1998. He receives four life sentences.

1996 Congress passes the Communication Decency Act to regulate obscene material on the Internet. Courts rule it unconstitutional, a violation of free speech protections.

1996 Congress passes the Antiterrorism and Effective Death Penalty Act, enhancing law enforcement capabilities in terrorism cases and banning U.S. citizens and companies from doing business with or supporting organizations designated as foreign terrorist organizations by the U.S. State Department.

1998 Henry C. Lee establishes the Henry C. Lee Institute of Forensic Science in order to advance the study and development of forensic science. In 1996 Lee receives the Medal of Justice from the Justice Foundation and in 1998 the Lifetime Achievement Award of the Science and Engineer Association.

May 1998 Having murdered his parents the day before, high school student **Kip Kinkel**, enters the cafeteria of Thurston High School in Springfield, Oregon, and opens fire, killing two students and wounding twenty-six others. He is convicted in 1999 of the four murders and of twenty-six counts of attempted murder.

April 1999 In Littleton, Colorado, Columbine High School seniors Eric Harris and Dylan Klebold bring an arsenal of weapons to school and open fire, wounding twenty-six students and killing thirteen people, including a teacher, before taking their own lives.

September 11, 2001 Terrorists of Middle Eastern origin crash three hijacked airliners into New York's World Trade Center and the Pentagon in Washington, D.C. A fourth hijacked airliner crashes in rural Pennsylvania on its way to a target. Almost 3,000 people are killed in the attacks.

March 2003 The U.S. Department of Homeland Security begins operation to combat terrorist threats.

Words to Know

A

Adjudication: The process of resolving an issue through a court decision.

Aggravated assault: An attack by one person upon another with intent to inflict severe bodily injury, usually by using a weapon.

AMBER Alert: (America's Missing: Broadcast Emergency Response) A national communications network for alerting the public immediately after the abduction of a youth under eighteen years of age has been reported and when the child is considered in danger. The alerts bring in the assistance of the local public in spotting the missing child or his or her abductor.

Appellate: Courts that do not hear original cases but review lower trial court decisions to determine if proper legal procedures were followed. Appeals are heard in front of a panel of judges without a jury.

Arraignment: A part of the criminal justice process during which the formal charges are read to the defendant. The defendant is advised of his or her rights, enters a plea of guilty or not guilty, and has bail and a trial date set.

Arson: Any intentional or malicious burning or attempt to burn a house, public building, motor vehicle or aircraft, or some other personal property of another person.

Assault: An attack that may or may not involve physical contact. Intentionally frightening a person or shouting threats could be considered assault.

B

Bail: Money paid for the temporary release of an arrested person and to guarantee that the accused will appear for trial.

Beyond reasonable doubt: A phrase referring to the need to determine a defendant's guilt with certainty. This level of certainty is required for criminal convictions.

Bill of Rights: The first ten amendments to the U.S. Constitution, adopted in 1791. The Bill of Rights includes various protections of civil liberties in the criminal justice system, including protection from cruel punishment, unreasonable search, and self-incrimination.

Biohazard: Any biological material that has the potential to cause harm to human beings or to the environment.

Black market: The illegal sale of goods in violation of government regulations, such as selling illegal liquor at very high prices.

Blasphemy: A colonial-era crime of showing a lack of reverence toward God.

Bootlegger: A person who illegally transports liquor.

Bullying: Behavior such as teasing and threats, exclusion from social activities, and more physical intimidation; a common form of behavior among juveniles.

Burglary: Forcefully entering a home to commit a crime.

C

Capital punishment: The execution of a criminal offender; also known as the death penalty.

Capitalism: An economic system in which private business and markets determine the prices, distribution, and production of goods largely without government intervention.

Child abuse: Causing physical or emotional harm to a child.

Child labor laws: Laws restricting the type of work children can do and the number of hours they can work. These laws are designed to protect children from dangerous, unsanitary factory and farm conditions and from long hours of work at low pay. Such laws also enable them to pursue an education.

Child neglect: A failure to provide a child's basic needs, including adequate food or shelter.

Child pornography: A felony criminal offense often involving photographing and videotaping nude children or children being sexually abused.

Chop shop: A place where stolen cars are taken apart and the parts individually sold.

Civil disobedience: Challenging rules of public behavior in a nonviolent manner.

Civil law: Laws regulating ordinary private matters, in contrast to criminal law.

Civil liberties: Certain basic protections from government interference offered by the U.S. Constitution, such as freedom from self-incrimination and freedom from unreasonable searches.

Common law: A legal system in use for several centuries in England that provides a set of judicial rules "commonly" applied to resolve similar disputes. Common law is built on a history of judge's decisions rather than relying on codes, or laws, passed by a legislature. The decisions are written down and compiled annually in legal volumes available for judges to refer to.

Communism: A political and economic system where a single party controls all aspects of citizens' lives and private ownership of property is banned.

Community-based corrections: Facilities, often located in neighborhoods, that allow convicted offenders to maintain normal family relationships and friendships while receiving rehabilitation services such as counseling, work training, and job placement.

Constable: A colonial policing figure who delivered warrants, supervised the volunteer night watchmen, and carried out the routine local government functions of the community.

Copyright: The legal right of an author, publisher, composer, or other person who creates a work to exclusively print, publish, distribute, or perform the work in public.

Coroner: A public official who investigates deaths that have not clearly resulted from natural causes.

Counterterrorism: A coordinated effort among many government agencies to fight and stop terrorism.

Court-martial: A court consisting of military personnel trying a case of another military person accused of violating military law.

Crime: A socially harmful act that is prohibited and punishable by criminal law.

Crime syndicate: A group of people who work together in an illegal business activity.

Criminal justice system: The loose collection of public agencies including the police, courts, and prison officials responsible for catching and arresting suspected criminals, determining their guilt, and imposing the sentence.

Criminology: The scientific study of criminal behavior to aid in preventing and solving crimes.

Cycle of violence: The tendency of people abused during childhood to commit abuse or other crimes as adults.

D

Defendant: A person accused of a crime.

Defense attorney: A lawyer who represents a defendant to provide him or her the best possible defense from the time of arrest through sentencing and, later, appeals of the case. The defense attorney is responsible for seeing that the constitutional rights of the defendant are protected.

Delinquents: Juveniles who commit acts considered adult crimes.

Democracy: A system of government that allows multiple political parties, the members of which are elected to various government offices by popular vote of the people.

Desertion: The military crime of abandoning a military post or assignment without approval.

Disposition: The legal term for a sentence in the criminal justice system; sentences may range from fines to imprisonment in a large, tightly guarded correctional facility.

Dissident: A person with opposing political views to those in power or the government.

DNA: DNA is deoxyribonucleic acid, the substance that chromosomes are made of. Chromosomes, long connected double strands of DNA that have a structure resembling a twisted ladder, contain an individual's genetic code, which is unique to every person (except identical twins, who share the same genetic code).

Double jeopardy: A rule stating that a person cannot be tried for the same offense twice.

Drug cartel: An organized crime group that grows and sells narcotics.

Drug trafficking: The buying or selling of illegal drugs.

E

Ecoterrorism: Terrorist activities that target businesses or other organizations that are thought to be damaging the environment. The term can also refer to terrorist actions designed to harm the environment of a political enemy.

Embezzlement: The stealing of money or property by a trusted employee or other person.

Encryption: The use of secret codes that can be translated into meaningful communications only by authorized persons who have knowledge of the code.

Environmental crime: To commit an act with intent to harm ecological or biological systems for the purpose of personal or corporate gain; actions that violate environmental protection laws.

Espionage: Spies acquiring information about the activities of another country.

Exclusionary rule: Evidence obtained illegally by the police cannot be used—will be excluded from consideration—in a court of law.

Extortion: Threats to commit violence or other types of harm with the intent of obtaining money or property from another person or group.

F

Felony: A serious crime that can lead to imprisonment or execution.

First-degree murder: A deliberate and planned killing; or, a murder in connection with the commission of another felony crime such as robbery or rape.

Forensic science: The application of a wide range of scientific knowledge within a court of law. Forensic science is used to analyze a crime scene, including weapon identification, fingerprinting, document analysis, chemical identification, and trace analysis of hair and fibers.

Forgery: The signing of a false name on a legal document such as a check, and the cashing of such a check at a store or bank using false identification.

Fraud: Intentionally deceiving another for personal economic benefit.

G

Grand jury: A group of citizens chosen from the community who determine in a hearing closed to the public if there is sufficient evidence to justify indictment of the accused and a trial. Only prosecutors present evidence in grand jury hearings, not attorneys representing the defendant.

Grand larceny: Theft of money or property of great value.

H

Habitual offender: A criminal who repeatedly commits crimes, often of various types.

Hacker: Someone who gains unauthorized access to a specific computer network system and reads or copies secret or private information.

Halfway house: Rigidly controlled rehabilitation homes for offenders who have been released early from prison or are on parole. Halfway houses were created to relieve prison overcrowding. Services can include counseling, treatment, and education programs, or halfway houses can simply be a place to live under supervision.

Hate crime: A violent attack against a person or group because of race, ethnicity, religion, or gender.

Hazardous waste: Any solid or liquid substance that because of its quantity, concentration, or physical or chemical properties may cause serious harm to humans or the environment when it is improperly transported, treated, stored, or disposed of.

Heresy: Holding a belief that conflicts with church doctrine. In some societies, during certain eras—such as colonial America—heresy has been prosecuted as a crime.

Hung jury: A circumstance wherein a jury cannot agree on a verdict; in such cases the defendant may face a retrial.

I

Identity theft: The theft of an individual's identifying information—including credit card numbers, social security number, or driver's license number—to allow a criminal to use another person's identity in making purchases or for other unauthorized activities.

Impartial jury: The notion that the members of jury will regard all evidence presented with an open mind.

Incarceration: Confining a person in jail or prison.

Indictment: A written accusation of criminal charges against a person.

Insider trading: Buying and selling securities based on reliable business information not available to the general public.

Insubordination: A military crime involving the disobeying of an authority, such as a military commander.

Intake worker: A person trained to work with youthful offenders, such as a probation officer.

Intellectual property (IP) theft: The theft of material that is copyrighted, the theft of trade secrets, and violations of trademarks.

Involuntary manslaughter: A homicide resulting from negligence or lack of regard for safety.

J

Jail: A facility operated by a city or county for short-term detention of defendants awaiting trial or those convicted of misdemeanors.

Jim Crow: State and local laws in the United States that enforced legal segregation in the first half of the twentieth century, keeping races separated in every aspect of life from schools to restrooms and water fountains. Such laws were particularly common in the South.

Jurisdiction: The geographic area or type of crime over which certain branches of law enforcement or courts have legal authority.

Juvenile courts: A special court system that has jurisdiction over children accused of criminal conduct, over youthful victims of abuse or neglect, and over young people who violate rules that apply only to juveniles.

L

Labor racketeering: The existence of a criminal organization that works its way into a position of power in a labor union in order to steal from the union's retirement and health funds.

Landmark decision: A ruling by the U.S. Supreme Court that sets an important precedent for future cases and can influence daily operating procedures of police, courts, and corrections.

Larceny: Theft of property, either with or without the use of force.

Loan sharking: Charging very high interest rates on loans.

M

Mafia: A crime organization originating in Sicily, Italy, that is thought to control racketeering in the United States.

Magistrate: In colonial times the magistrate was the key judicial official in local courts, often a key member of the community. In modern times, a magistrate is an official with limited judicial authority who issues arrest and search warrants, sets bail, conducts pretrial hearings, and hears misdemeanor cases.

Mail fraud: Using the mail system to make false offers to or otherwise defraud recipients.

Malice: The intent to inflict serious bodily harm.

Mandatory sentence: A specific penalty required by law upon conviction for a specific offense.

Manslaughter: A homicide not involving malice, or the intent to inflict serious harm.

Martial law: A legal system through which the military exerts police power in place of civilian rule in politically unstable areas to protect safety and property.

Mass murderer: A person who kills many people in a single crime episode.

Mediation: A process for resolving disputes in which both the victim and offender must agree to meet and attempt to settle their dispute in a face-to-face manner, under the guidance of a neutral party.

Midnight dumping: The illegal disposal of hazardous wastes under cover of darkness in a remote area.

Miranda rights: The rights of a defendant to obtain legal counsel and refrain from self-incrimination.

Misdemeanor: A minor crime usually punishable by brief jail time or a fine.

Mistrial: A circumstance whereby a trial is discontinued because of a serious mistake or misconduct on the part of attorneys, court officials, or jury members.

Money laundering: To make the tracking of crime profits very difficult by placing money gained from crime into legitimate financial institutions, often banks outside the United States; placing such money into accounts of bogus companies; or mixing such funds with legally obtained money in the bank accounts of legitimate companies owned or operated by organized crime groups.

Moral values: The commonly accepted standards of what is right and wrong.

Multiple homicide: A crime in which a person kills more than one person on a single occasion.

Murder: Killing another person with malicious intent.

N

Narcotic: Habit-forming drugs that relieve pain or cause sleep, including heroin and opium.

Neighborhood watch: A crime prevention program in which residents watch out for suspicious activity in their neighborhoods and notify the police if they spot criminal activity.

O

Obscene: Material that has no socially redeeming value and is considered offensive according to community standards of decency.

Organized crime: People or groups joined together to profit from illegal businesses.

Organized labor: A collective effort by workers and labor organizations in general to seek better working conditions.

P

Page-jacking: A fake Web site using the same key words or Web site descriptions as a legitimate site with the intention of misdirecting Internet traffic to another site such as a pornography site.

Paraphilia: Sexual behavior considered bizarre or abnormal, such as voyeurism (spying on others for sexual pleasure) or pedophilia (sexual desire involving children).

Parens patriae: The concept that the government has the right to become the parent of children in need—to save them from terrible living conditions or protect them from criminal influences.

Parole: The release of an inmate before the end of his or her sentence.

Pedophilia: Receiving sexual pleasure from activities that focus on children as sex objects.

Penitentiary or prison: A state or federal facility for holding inmates convicted of a felony.

Perjury: Intentionally making a false statement or lying while under oath during a court appearance.

Petition: Requesting to be heard by the courts on some dispute.

Petty larceny: Theft of small amounts of money.

Pillory: A form of colonial-period punishment consisting of a wooden frame that has holes for heads and hands.

Plea bargain: A guilty plea offered by the defendant in return for reduced charges, a lighter sentence, or some other consideration.

Pollutant: A man-made waste that contaminates the environment.

Pornography: Materials such as magazines, books, pictures, and videos that show nudity and sexual acts.

Prejudice: A judgment or opinion formed without sufficient information.

Preponderance of evidence: A sufficient amount of evidence to indicate the guilt of the accused. The term also refers to the level of evidence used in civil cases and juvenile courts.

Price-fixing: Governments or companies artificially setting the price for particular goods rather than letting the market determine pricing.

Probable cause: Sufficient evidence to support an arrest.

Probation: A criminal sentence other than jail or prison time for persons convicted of less serious crimes; those sentenced with probation are usually placed under court supervision for a specific period of time.

Prohibition: Prohibiting the production, sale, transport, and possession of alcoholic beverages resulting from the adoption of the Eighteenth Amendment to the U.S. Constitution in 1919 and the resulting Volstead Act of 1920; this amendment was repealed by the Twenty-first Amendment to the Constitution in December in 1933.

Property crimes: Theft where no force or threat of force is directed toward an individual; such crimes are usually driven by the prospect of financial gain.

Prosecutor: Public officials who represent the government in criminal cases. Prosecutors are often known as district attorneys or prosecuting attorneys in federal courts and are commonly elected or appointed to their positions.

Prostitution: A person offering sexual acts in return for payments, generally payments of money.

Public defender: A state-employed attorney who provides free legal counsel to defendants too poor to hire a lawyer.

Public order crime: Behavior that is banned because it threatens the general well-being of a community or society.

R

Racism: To be prejudiced against people of a different race.

Racketeering: The act of participating in a continuing pattern of criminal behavior.

Rape: Having sexual relations by force or the threat of force.

Rehabilitation: Providing treatment to an offender to prevent further criminal behavior.

Restitution: Compensation or payment by an offender to a victim; restitution may involve community service work rather than incarceration or payments.

Restraining trade: An effort to inhibit business competition through illegal means, such as fixing prices of goods and services artificially low.

Robbery: Taking money or property by force or the threat of force.

S

Sabotage: To destroy military or industrial facilities.

Second-degree murder: An unplanned or accidental killing through a desire to cause serious bodily harm.

Securities: Stocks or bonds.

Securities fraud: An individual or organization falsely manipulating the market price of a stock or commodity by deliberately providing misleading information to investors.

Self-incrimination: Offering damaging information about oneself during a trial or hearing; a person cannot be made to testify against him or herself and has the right to remain silent during a trial or interrogation.

Serial killer: A person who kills multiple people over a period of time.

Shield laws: Legislation prohibiting rape victims from being questioned about their prior sexual history unless specific need for the information is identified.

Shoplifting: A common form of petty larceny; taking merchandise from a store without paying for it.

Slave patrols: Groups of white volunteers assembled in the 1740s to police the black slave populations with the intent of protecting white citizens from slaves, suppressing slave uprisings, and capturing runaway slaves. Slave patrols are considered an early form of organized policing.

Sociopathic: A personality disorder characterized by antisocial, often destructive, behavior with little show of emotion.

Sovereignty: A government largely free from outside political control.

Speakeasy: A place where alcoholic beverages were illegally sold during Prohibition.

Stalking: The act of repeatedly following or spying on another person or making unwanted communications or threats.

Status offenses: Rules that apply only to juveniles such as unapproved absence from school (truancy), running away from home, alcohol and tobacco use, and refusing to obey parents.

Statutory rape: Rape without force involving an adult and teenager under the age of consent who has apparently agreed to the act; it is a crime because it is established by statute, or law.

Stranger violence: A crime in which the victim has had no previous contact with his or her attacker.

Strike: A work stoppage intended to force an employer to meet worker demands.

Subversive: Political radicals working secretly to overthrow a government.

Supermax prisons: Short for super-maximum-security prisons. Supermax prisons are designed to keep the most violent or disruptive inmates separated from other prisoners and correction staff, often in a special area within an existing prison.

T

Temperance: The use of alcoholic beverages in moderation or abstinence from all alcohol.

Terrorism: The planned use of force or violence, normally against innocent civilians, to make a statement about a cause. Terrorist attacks are staged for maximum surprise, shock, and destruction to influence individuals, groups, or governments to give in to certain demands.

Three-strikes laws: Laws that dictate that a criminal convicted of his or her third felony must remain in prison for an extended period of time, sometimes for life.

Toxicity: The degree to which a substance is poisonous.

Toxicology: The study of toxic or poisonous substances that can cause harm or death to any individual who takes them, depending on the amount ingested.

Trace evidence: Microscopic or larger materials, commonly hairs or fibers, transferred from person to person or object to object during a crime; examples include human or animal hair as well as wood, clothing, or carpet fibers.

Treason: An attempt to overthrow one's own government.

True crime: Stories in books, magazines, or films or on television programs that are based on actual crimes.

Trusts: Organizations formed by combining several major industries together to stifle competition and run smaller companies out of business.

V

Victim compensation: Payment of funds to help victims survive the financial losses caused by crimes against them.

Victimization: The physical, emotional, and financial harm victims suffer from crime, including violent crime, property crime, and business corruption.

Victimless crime: Crimes often between two persons who agree to the activity, leaving no immediate victims to file charges; such crimes are considered crimes against society and are defined by law or statute.

Victims' rights: A guarantee that victims of crime be treated with dignity and fairness by police, prosecutors, and other officials and be protected from threats and harm; victims may be notified about the progress of their case and informed of upcoming court dates such as parole hearings.

Vigilantes: A group of citizens assembled on their own initiative to maintain order.

Violent crime: Crimes against the person including murder, robbery, aggravated assault, rape, sniper attacks, crimes of hate, and stalking.

Virus: A computer program that disrupts or destroys existing computer systems by destroying computer files. Viruses often cost companies and individuals millions of dollars in downtime.

W

Warrant: An order issued by a judge or magistrate to make an arrest, seize property, or make a search.

White-collar crime: A person using a position of authority and responsibility in a legitimate business organization to commit crimes of fraud and deceit for his or her personal financial gain.

Work release: The release of selected inmates from a prison or community residential center for work during the day, returning at night.

Crime and Punishment in America

BIOGRAPHIES

Jane Addams

Born September 6, 1860 (Cedarville, Illinois)
Died May 21, 1935 (Chicago, Illinois)

Social reformer

By the early 1900s Jane Addams was one of the most famous and respected women in America. Her practical approach to charity, business, and reform worked well within the American free enterprise system (the freedom of private businesses to operate competitively for profit with minimal government regulation). Through her social activism to assist the poor and the young, Addams inspired the creation of the Illinois juvenile justice system, the first in the nation. The Illinois state system served as a model for other states and the federal government.

Addams also focused on pacifism (opposing war and violence) to promote nonviolent solutions to problems. She pursued her humanitarian work for a better American society throughout her lifetime. In 1931 Addams became the first American woman to receive the Nobel Peace Prize. The prize recognized her commitment to social reform and her work to promote peace in the world.

Based in part on her influence on the U.S. criminal justice system, in 1912 Addams became the first woman to make a nominating speech at a national political convention. She

"When a great party pledges itself to the protection of children, to the care of the aged, to the relief of overworked girls, to the safe-guarding of burdened men, it is inevitable that it should appeal to women."

1

Jane Addams. *(© Bettmann/Corbis)*

seconded the nomination of presidential candidate Theodore
Roosevelt (1858–1919; served 1901–09). A staunch supporter
of women's suffrage (right to vote), Addams served as vice
president of the National American Suffrage Alliance from
1911 to 1914. In 1913, seven years before the Nineteenth
Amendment to the U.S. Constitution granted women the right
to vote, Addams helped secure the vote for women in local
Chicago elections.

In 1915 Addams was the first woman to organize and
chair a Women's Peace Party in the United States. She was
cofounder of the Women's International League for Peace

and Freedom and served as its president for many years. Another direct influence on criminal justice came in 1920, when she helped found the American Civil Liberties Union (ACLU).

The ACLU became a leading organization in protecting the rights of defendants in the criminal justice process by a variety of actions, including raising public awareness, funding defense lawyers, and initiating test cases or joining existing cases. Addams served on its national committee for a decade. Popular as a lecturer and writer, many organizations sought Addams's participation. Between 1904 and 1935, she received honorary degrees from fifteen universities. In 1910 she was the first woman to receive an honorary degree from Yale University in New Haven, Connecticut.

A concern for fellow citizens

Jane Addams was born in 1860 in Cedarville, Illinois. Also called Jenny, she was the youngest of eight children born to Sarah Weber and John Huy Addams, a personal friend of President Abraham Lincoln (1809–1865; served 1861–65). Her family followed the Quaker faith (Christians opposed to war, oathtaking, and rituals) and valued hard work, a simple lifestyle, and social change through peaceful efforts.

Jane was just two when her mother died, leaving her father to raise her and her siblings. John Addams was a Republican state senator and an abolitionist (person opposed to slavery) and became the primary intellectual and moral influence in Jane's life. Jane suffered physically throughout her life with a painful curved spine, which caused her to walk pigeon-toed, with the toes turned inward. It made her very self-conscious about her appearance. Academically, she was an outstanding student and graduated from high school in 1877.

Jane next studied at Rockford Female Seminary in Rockford, Illinois, one of the oldest institutions for female education in the area. While at Rockford, Jane and a friend became concerned about the place of women in American society. They successfully lobbied the seminary to offer course work equivalent to that of men's colleges. Jane served as class president all four years at Rockford and in 1881 was valedictorian (top student of her graduating class).

Only a few months after her graduation, Jane's father died suddenly of a ruptured appendix. Jane was devastated by his untimely death, though left a very wealthy woman. She decided to pursue her plan of attending the Woman's Medical College of Pennsylvania in Philadelphia. During her first year, Jane's spinal condition forced her to undergo back surgery and withdraw from her studies. She spent the next several years in recovery while traveling throughout Europe. She returned to the United States in 1885 and settled in Baltimore, Maryland.

War on poverty

Addams journeyed back to Europe in 1887 with her former college classmate, Ellen Gates Starr. In Europe Addams was introduced to the idea of social settlements. These settlements were organized to recreate the conditions of village life within the neighborhoods of a city. In London, she observed the work of Toynbee Hall, a pioneering English settlement house designed to assist the poor. It was an experiment in social reform where Oxford University men resided and socialized along with the poor in London's East End. Addams embraced the settlement idea, since she was deeply disturbed by the urban poverty of the United States.

Addams believed social settlements in the United States would satisfy two needs. First, American cities had large numbers of immigrants who needed help adjusting to life in a big city. Second, she believed many educated and socially favored young people living in the cities needed to use their energies to serve others. Addams liked the idea that the settlement houses benefited both the poor and the favored. She was interested in providing an outlet for the talent and energy of college educated young people, but she also sincerely wanted to help those trapped by poverty. Addams and Starr agreed they would start a settlement in Chicago where Starr had been teaching school and had many friends.

Addams gave speeches in the Chicago area promoting the project while seeking support for settlement housing. Initially most listeners were curious why two well-educated young women planned to live in the slums of Chicago. The cause, however, seemed compassionate and gained support from church groups, civic organizations, and philanthropists (those who give money to good causes).

By the fall of 1889 Addams and Starr had rented a formerly elegant old house on Halsted Street called Hull House. They convinced several women to join them as residents and volunteers in serving a large immigrant community in the surrounding tenements on Chicago's West Side. It was agreed that Addams would be head resident. This decision was partly because her wealth was paying the costs of starting the settlement and also because she was financially self-sufficient through inheritance. She had the time and means to run Hull House.

Soon many socially advanced young ladies mingled with all classes of people without hesitation at Hull House. In the beginning, the women simply responded to the immediate needs of the community. Before long, the house provided classes, clubs, and lectures. Addams and Starr developed a wide circle of influential supporters, and a wide variety of speakers brought their expertise to teach fine arts and literature, as well as practical classes on child and health care. Addams developed educational, cultural, and medical programs for the community while lobbying for improved housing, fair labor practices, and just treatment for immigrants, the poor, and children within the country's criminal justice system.

Juvenile justice

Addams argued for a separate legal system for juveniles that would guide and teach them the proper way to behave rather than just locking them away in jails. Some supported the idea for the sake of the children, while others feared the growing number of immigrant street youth in Chicago in the late nineteenth century. In spite of the fears, Illinois became the first state to establish a separate court system for juveniles in 1899.

In the new juvenile courts, specially trained judges had enormous flexibility to act on a child's behalf, taking over for parents. The law defined a juvenile as a person less than sixteen years of age. Rather than prosecute a juvenile for a crime, the court would place the juvenile in a reform school or with foster parents. These juveniles remained under court supervision until the of age twenty-one. By 1925 almost all of the states had juvenile systems, using Illinois as a model.

A group of children stands in front of Hull House in Chicago, Illinois. Jane Addams helped establish and run Hull House, which provided classes, clubs, lectures, and other services to the poor members of the community. *(AP/Wide World Photos)*

As her reputation and influence grew, Addams was drawn into greater areas of civic responsibility. In 1905 she was appointed to Chicago's Board of Education. When the National Association for the Advancement of Colored People (NAACP) was formed in 1909, Addams was a member of its executive committee. The NAACP became a champion of justice for minorities. Also in 1909, Addams became the first woman to be elected president of the National Conference of Charities and Correction, later known as the National Conference of Social Work. In 1911 she became the first head of the National Federation of Settlements, an organization she remained a part of until she died.

Peace activist

Jane Addams was dubbed by some in the media as "the only American saint." Her outspoken pacifist stance during World War I, however, nearly destroyed her reputation. Shaped by her Quaker upbringing, since the early 1900s Addams had been involved in the peace movement. In 1915 she was invited to participate in the International Congress of Women at The Hague, Netherlands.

After returning, Addams delivered a speech at Carnegie Hall in New York City on July 9, 1915, in which she questioned nationalism (exceptionally strong support of one's own nation above all others) and support for war. She also criticized the glorification of war itself. Addams encouraged the public to recognize the futility of war and support other ways to resolve international disputes.

Addams was surprised by the strong negative reactions of the media and the public to her speech. She maintained her pacifist views even when the United States entered the war in 1917. Addams suddenly found herself used as a symbol of those considered disloyal to America and was cast in the role of national villain.

Addams regained a small measure of public respect in 1918 when she toured the United States on behalf of President Herbert Hoover's (1874–1964; served 1929–33) Department of Food Administration and lectured women on domestic efforts needed during the war. Addams spent much of the 1920s, however, in Europe and Asia working on behalf of the Women's International League for Peace and Freedom.

Addams also spoke out against intolerance. She called for a civilized approach to the problems facing America and the world. The media, however, once again criticized her when she pleaded for food relief for starving civilians in the defeated countries of Europe after the war ended. She also defended the legal rights of those arrested during the postwar Red Scare, the American government and public fear of communism and its perceived threat to American democracy that led to mass arrests of foreigners.

Addams considered free speech to be the greatest characteristic of the United States. As a result she helped found the American Civil Liberties Union in 1920 to ensure every person's right to believe and speak as he or she chose. Pacifists (those who believed in peace and would not fight in wars) and those who advocated social welfare were often connected with socialism (a society in which no one owns private property, but rather, the government or public owns all goods and the means of distributing them among the people) and communism in the United States. Because of her leadership on social issues at the time, Addams was attacked by some as a revolutionary and military intelligence labeled Addams as a "questionable" American.

With the 1930s bringing the Great Depression (1929–41; a time of economic crisis and high unemployment that began with the stock market crash in 1929) and the threat of a new war in Europe, Addams's pacifism seemed more reasonable rather than revolutionary. Isolationism (opposition to involvement in foreign wars) dominated the public's mood. With millions of Americans suffering economic hardships from the Depression, her achievements in social reform were once again viewed as an invaluable contribution to American society.

Jane Addams lived and worked out of Hull House until her death from intestinal cancer on May 21, 1935. She lay in state at Hull House for two days while thousands of mourners filed past her coffin. She was buried in the old family cemetery at Cedarville, Illinois.

For More Information

Books

Addams, Jane. *The Second Twenty Years at Hull House*. New York: Macmillan, 1930.

Davis, Allen F. *American Heroine: The Life and Legend of Jane Addams*. New York: Oxford University Press, 1973.

Felder, Deborah G. *The 100 Most Influential Women of All Time: A Ranking Past and Present*. New York: Citadel Press, 1996.

Kelley, Colleen E., and Anna L. Eblen, eds. *Women Who Speak for Peace*. Lanham, MD: Rowman and Littlefield Publishers, Inc., 2002.

Web Sites

"1889 Jane Addams Hull House." *Chicago Public Library.* http://www. chipublib.org/004chicago/timeline/hullhouse.html (accessed on August 15, 2004).

"Jane Addams—Biography." *Nobel e-Museum.* http://www.nobel.se/peace/ laureates/1931/addams-bio.html (accessed on August 15, 2004).

Urban Experience in Chicago: Hull-House and Its Neighborhoods, 1889–1963. http://www.uic.edu/jaddams/hull/urbanexp/ (accessed on August 15, 2004).

Gustave de Beaumont

Born February 6, 1802 (Beaumont-la-Chartre, France)
Died February 22, 1866 (Paris, France)

French magistrate, prison reformer

"But while working on the penitentiary system we shall see America; in visiting its prisons we shall be visiting its inhabitants, its cities, its institutions, its customs."

Gustave de Beaumont was a nineteenth-century French statesman when he received a commission from the King of France Louis Phillipe (1773–1850) to inspect American prison systems for the French government. In 1831 Beaumont and his friend and noted historian Alexis de Tocqueville (1805–1859) sailed to the United States. They spent nine months inspecting American prisons. At the completion of their study, they published a report entitled *On the Penitentiary System in the United States and Its Application to France.*

America was the New World to Europeans in the 1830s. The French Revolution (1789–99; a war in which the monarchy was overthrown and a republic was established) had called for "liberty, equality and fraternity," and the United States was seen as the political future with its principles based in individualism and equality. Many Europeans came to North America to observe and write accounts during these years. But the experiences of Beaumont and Tocqueville—in observing the U.S. criminal justice system—would greatly affect the thinking of the Western world.

French aristocracy

Gustave de Beaumont was born in France in 1802, a few months after the dictatorship of Napoleon Bonaparte (1769–1821) began. The youngest son of Jules de Beaumont and Rose Preau de la Baraudiere, Gustave and his three siblings grew up comfortably on the farm of Chateau de la Borde. The countryside they called home was near the town of Beaumont-la-Chartre, where their father served as mayor. The town was located in the province of Sarthe, a rural and politically volatile region of France.

The aristocratic (wealthy upper class) Beaumont family had a long tradition of loyalty to the king. When the dictatorship of Napoleon ended in 1814, the Bourbon dynasty returned to the monarchy of France under the reign of King Louis XVIII (1755–1824). Young Gustave completed his schooling and went on to study law. When he reached the age of eligibility, he was appointed as an apprentice magistrate (local judge) in the courts because of his family's loyalty.

About this time, Gustave met another young magistrate who was to become a lifelong friend. Three years his junior, Alexis de Tocqueville was as idealistic and ambitious as Beaumont. Together the young nobles plunged into an intense course of studies including English, philosophy, history, and politics.

Charles X (1757–1836) ascended the throne in 1824 and a crisis began brewing in France. The storm broke on July 25, 1830, in the form of the French Revolution. The Bourbon dynasty was once again in exile and Charles X, who was the last Bourbon king of France, left for England three days later. Louis Philippe ascended the throne as the head of the House of Orleans. He was from the line of kings who had originally taken the monarchy from the Bourbons. Public loyalties were immediately divided.

Beaumont was in Paris at the time of the Revolution and survived the battle as well as the ensuing politics. He and Tocqueville retained their jobs as magistrates but both men found themselves in a dilemma. Like most nobility they were caught between the requirements of the new monarchy and loyalty to the Bourbon dynasty and family traditions.

A lithograph of Alexis de Tocqueville, friend and associate of Gustave de Beaumont. French government officials, Beaumont and Tocqueville went to America to conduct research on the prison system as a way of escaping the turmoil of the French Revolution as well as study the new democratic government and culture of the United States. *(The Library of Congress)*

Political play

The new government wanted to determine the commitment of its administrators and, after dismissing its known enemies, asked all remaining officials to take the oath of allegiance to Louis Philippe. Beaumont and Tocqueville reluctantly took the oath, which greatly bothered the majority of their friends and family—most of whom had refused to take the oath and had resigned instead of compromising their loyalties.

Despite their show of commitment, the government still suspected the dedication of the magistrates and they operated under a cloud of suspicion. Their higher position in society had made life intolerable since the Revolution, and to make matters worse public protests were becoming increasingly serious throughout the country. The continuing government of Louis Philippe was not assured, and if the government did fall the magistrates oath of allegiance had compromised them with whoever might gain the throne.

The political climate in France left twenty-eight-year-old Beaumont uneasy about his future prospects. He discussed his concerns with Tocqueville and on October 31, 1830, they submitted a formal request to the government to study the new prison reforms taking place in the United States. Both men were anxious to see the country they had heard so much about and to examine democracy in action.

Both men needed clearance from two ministries of the French government to obtain a leave of absence from their duties for the trip. They finally received permission for the eighteen-month assignment, but were required to travel at their own expense. Their departure date was set for April 1, 1831. They spent months preparing for their journey as well as studying the English language.

Coming to America

The United States in 1831 consisted of all lands east of the Mississippi River and lands to the west considered part of the 828,000-square-mile acquisition from France known as the Louisiana Purchase in 1803. The estimated population of thirteen million persons lived mostly along the East Coast. Beaumont and Tocqueville set sail from Le Havre, France, on April 3 aboard the *Havre*. After more than a month at sea they had their first glimpse of America when they landed in Newport, Rhode Island, on May 9.

Their original destination had been New York City but adverse weather and a shortage of food and water had forced an early landing in Rhode Island. They spent the night onboard ship and left Newport the next day on an American steamboat that delivered them to New York City on May 11. During their time in America the men used a wide variety of transportation including stagecoaches, canoes, sailing ships, and horseback.

Conscious of their official purpose, Beaumont and Tocqueville immediately began their investigation of American prisons. They arrived at Mount Pleasant, New York, on May 29 to visit Sing Sing Prison where they began their report, entitled *On the Penitentiary System in the United States and Its Application to France* (see sidebar). They based their report on a thorough study of the reforms at Sing Sing, as well as at Auburn in New York, Cherry Hill in Philadelphia, and Wethersfield in Connecticut. Because their interests only involved the new penitentiary system, they spent little time on the older prisons that existed in most American states. Included in the report were interviews with wardens, supervisors, and prisoners. They wrote about the makeup of the prison population as well as the practices and attitudes about punishment. Armed with his sketch books, Beaumont documented much in pictures while Tocqueville wrote in his journals.

Beaumont and Tocqueville were dedicated to their prison assignment but also used their research to make observations

The Prison Report

Gustave de Beaumont and Alexis de Tocqueville coauthored a volume on prison reform entitled *On the Penitentiary System in the United States and Its Application to France*. Published in 1833, it covered their research of American penal systems conducted from May 1831 through February 1832. The report written by Beaumont and Tocqueville observed that while some American penitentiaries in their study could serve as models for other countries to copy, some were models of everything that should be avoided.

The two facilities Beaumont and Tocqueville studied most thoroughly were the Cherry Hill Prison in Philadelphia and the Auburn Prison in New York. They found three distinct differences that set them apart from older American prisons and from European prisons. First, isolation was used in order to keep prisoners from corrupting each other. Secondly, work was provided for inmates throughout their jail time. Lastly, an attempt was made by authorities to reform prisoners both morally and spiritually.

They reported that nine states had adopted new systems and the other fifteen still used the old systems. The old systems were overcrowded and unhealthy with many escapes and deaths recorded. Of those states using the new systems, most followed Auburn, which showed some evidence of changing criminals. At Auburn isolation was enforced by forbidding inmates to talk to one another even while working together during the day. At night, each inmate was locked in a separate cell to avoid communication.

Beaumont carried several notebooks to record the journey in sketches. The first album was a rough sketchbook done in pencil to record his first impression of the people and places he saw. The second album was produced in pen and ink, reproducing the pencil sketches in more elaborate detail for the report.

about American democracy and culture in general. The tireless travelers covered a large area in their brief time in North America. They went north through the Great Lakes to Canada and back south as far as New Orleans before heading to Washington, D.C. Along the way they stopped and spoke to politicians, businessmen, commentators, and newsmen.

The media took note of the two French gentlemen who had been commissioned by the King of France and gave them wide coverage in the press. While in Washington, D.C., Beaumont and Tocqueville met with U.S. president Andrew Jackson (1767–1845; served 1829–37) and former president John

Quincy Adams (1767–1848; served 1825–29). Beaumont and Tocqueville were summoned back to France early, after having been absent less than a year. They obediently returned to New York City and set sail aboard the *Havre* on February 20, 1832.

Political disappointment

Upon their arrival in Paris at the end of March, the two friends found the government unwelcoming and there was a cholera (an infectious, often fatal disease of the intestines) epidemic threatening the city. Within two months of their return Beaumont had been dismissed from his post in the government courts and Tocqueville resigned in protest. They kept busy by writing their prison report. It was published early in 1833 in both of their names. Beaumont wrote the main text and provided the sketches for the report. Tocqueville provided footnotes and comments and inspected several French prisons to complete their research.

The men agreed to go their separate ways in further writings about their American experiences. As it turned out, their report, as well as their individual writings, were well received. Tocqueville wrote the widely acclaimed *Democracy in America* and Beaumont published a novel titled *Marie.* The novel was based on ethnic relations he had observed in the United States, especially between black and white Americans. Beaumont received national acclaim for the novel as it went through five editions.

In 1836 Beaumont married his cousin, Clementine de Lafayette, who was the granddaughter of the French hero Marquis de Lafayette (1757–1834). Beaumont went to Ireland and gathered information for a second case study that was published in 1839. He turned to national politics in 1840 and was elected to a legislative role in the Chamber of Deputies. Beaumont remained in politics including a term as ambassador to England until his death in Paris on February 22, 1866.

For More Information

Books

Hall, Kermit. *Oxford Companion to American Law.* New York: Oxford University Press, 2002.

Levinson, David, ed. *Encyclopedia of Crime and Punishment.* Thousand Oaks, CA: Sage Publications, Inc., 2002.

McCarthy, Eugene, J. *America Revisited: 150 Years After Tocqueville.* Garden City, NY: Doubleday & Company, Inc., 1978.

Pierson, George Wilson. *Tocqueville and Beaumont in America.* New York: Oxford University Press, 1938.

Web Site

The Alexis de Tocqueville Tour: Exploring Democracy in America. http://www.tocqueville.org (accessed on August 15, 2004).

Ivan Boesky

Born March 6, 1937 (Detroit, Michigan)

Wall Street financier, white-collar criminal

Ivan Boesky worked in the fast-paced, high stakes world of Wall Street investing during the suddenly lucrative years of the 1980s. He was a financier who built a highly successful business by trading stock in companies experiencing financial difficulties. Boesky, however, became involved in a financial scam using "insider trading" (buying and selling stocks based on information not available to the general public), amounting to billions of dollars. Boesky was caught and put on trial, and the country was shocked by the extent of stock related thefts revealed during the government's investigation of Boesky and other financiers. For his crimes in the insider trading scandal Boesky paid fines, served prison time, and was banned from the securities (stocks and bonds) industry for life.

"Greed is all right, by the way. I want you to know that. I think greed is healthy. You can be greedy and still feel good about yourself."

A golden opportunity

Ivan Frederick Boesky was born in Detroit, Michigan, in 1937. His father, William H. Boesky, had immigrated to America from Ykaterinoslav, Russia, in 1912. William ran a chain of bars in Detroit. Ivan spent two years at Cranbrook, a prestigious prep school (private school where students prepare for

Ivan Boesky. *(© Bettmann/Corbis)*

college) outside of Detroit where he distinguished himself as an outstanding wrestler. He graduated from an inner-city school called Mumford High and went on to several colleges but never completed a degree.

Ivan eventually enrolled at the Detroit College of Law, which did not require a college degree for admission. He graduated in 1964. While working as a law clerk for a federal district court judge in 1960, Ivan met Selma Silberstein and they married. Soon after they had their first child, Billy, and in 1966 they moved to New York City where Ivan started a new career trading stocks.

In his thirties, Ivan had found work at several securities firms on Wall Street but had little success. As a result he decided to start his own trading firm. With financial help from his in-laws, he opened and was managing partner for the Ivan F. Boesky Corporation in 1975. Boesky's specialty was trading stock in companies targeted by other companies for takeover. The companies were typically in trouble financially and their stock values had fallen. A takeover by a healthy company, however, would often send the stock prices soaring. Boesky's success in speculating on these stocks made him one of the richest traders on Wall Street by the 1980s. In 1981 he became chairman and chief executive officer of the Boesky Corp.

Boesky developed a working relationship with Drexel Burnham Lambert, a New York investment bank where Dennis Levine was a managing editor and Michael Milken (1946–; see sidebar) was a financial executive. Boesky and Levine made a deal in which Boesky would pay a percentage of his profits to Levine for insider tips on upcoming company mergers, trades, or takeovers. This highly illegal activity is called insider trading.

White-collar crime

Insider trading occurs when any person on Wall Street receives confidential information about the movement of stocks or planned mergers and acquisitions. The person then takes that information and uses or trades it for personal gain. In 1934 the federal government set up the Security Exchange Commission (SEC) to regulate Wall Street. The SEC made it illegal for anyone to act on insider information; if a person receives "insider" knowledge of some sort, he or she is required to keep this information secret and not act upon it. Wall Street was booming in the 1980s, but some wanted more—those participating in illegal activities included everyone from bankers and lawyers to major investors and stockbrokers.

Boesky and his partners not only profited from insider information, but they were able to manipulate the market value of stock prices through the formation of limited partnerships to further increase their earnings. Boesky's strategy was to create a limited company with capital (money) provided by partners, then pay more than the current trading price for that

Michael Milken, The Junk Bond King

For generations the American bond market has been dominated by two large bond rating agencies, Moody's and Standard & Poor's. The agencies rate a corporation's risk factors in order to help guide investors on Wall Street. Companies trying to attract investors are given a rating and are divided into two categories—either investment grade or below-investment grade bonds.

A "AAA" rating is risk-free and given to top, blue-chip corporations. Risk-free bonds usually yield very low interest rates to investors. BBB is the lowest credit rating considered to be a worthy investment grade. Below BBB are the speculative or high-yield bonds Wall Street called "fallen angels," because their companies had fallen on hard economic times. These bonds pay high interest and are sold at a discount because of their high risk factor. The fallen angel name stood until the 1970s when Michael Milken arrived on Wall Street.

Milken became known as the "Junk Bond King" because he made his fortune trading in the high-yield, low-grade bonds, which he nicknamed "junk bonds." In 1973 Milken started with two million dollars in capital at his company, Drexel Burnham Lambert, in New York City. He had found buyers for his own company's bonds by sharing his vision of the untapped market.

Milken soon generated a 100-percent return of the money invested in his company.

The next year Milken received double the amount of capital from his growing roster of clients, since they had made handsome returns on their investment. While other Wall Street traders tried to copy Milken, few could match his success. Impressed with Milken's achievements, additional investors contacted him and he soon accounted for most of Drexel's profits. In 1978 Milken moved his branch of Drexel from New York to Beverly Hills, California.

In the late 1970s corporate raiders were buying struggling companies and selling off pieces of those businesses and their assets at a huge gain. Milken transformed the art of speculating on these corporate takeovers with his ability to raise large amounts of capital using high-yield junk bonds. He knew the market and could raise capital for investors on short notice, but his methods were not always legal. Milken himself received huge bonuses from his company. One year he earned a total of $550 million.

Milken's involvement with insider trading practices became a focus of the SEC investigation in 1986 when Ivan Boesky agreed to be a government informer as part of his plea bargain. In September 1988, the SEC filed charges against Drexel and

Michael Milken. *(AP/Wide World Photos)*

Michael Milken under the 1970 RICO (Racketeer Influenced and Corrupt Organizations) statute. The SEC accused the defendants of trading on inside information as well as filing false disclosure forms with the SEC to disguise stock ownership.

Drexel and Milken were accused of manipulating stock prices, of keeping false records, and of defrauding their own clients. Drexel plead guilty to six felony counts of securities fraud on December 21 and paid a $650 million settlement fee. The company also agreed to assist in the indictment against Milken. Two months later, Milken was indicted on ninety-eight counts, including insider trading and racketeering.

In a plea bargain, Milken agreed to plead guilty to six charges of securities fraud and related charges while the government agreed to drop the more serious charges of insider trading and racketeering. On April 14, 1990, Milken was sentenced to ten years in prison and fined $600 million. He entered the minimum-security prison at Pleasanton, California, in 1991, but was released two years later when he was diagnosed with prostate cancer.

Michael Milken was seen as a financial visionary who could have influenced corporate restructuring in America without breaking the law. Instead, his manipulation of stocks and company buyouts resulted in a large number of bankruptcies, especially for small- and medium-sized companies. The corporate consolidations and layoffs resulting from the Drexel's high volume of takeovers left few defenders once the investigation caught up with the firm.

The resulting investigations and indictments also resulted in a loss of investor confidence in the nation's financial markets for years. Investors returned to traditional blue-chip stocks and mutual funds until enough time had passed and confidence returned to the riskier junk bonds. Following the insider trading scandal, Congress increased criminal penalties for securities violations.

company's shares which in turn brought in other investors believing the stock's potential. As a result of the buying, the stock value would rise and Boesky would sell his stock at the inflated prices, splitting the profits among the limited partners.

By the mid-1980s most of Boesky's capital resulted from his close association with Michael Milken of Drexel Burnham Lambert. Boesky, Milken, and others involved in the insider trading and market manipulations accumulated extraordinary fortunes from their criminal activities. Sophisticated schemes were necessary to conceal their deceit. They set up secret bank accounts to hide their money and misled federal regulators attempting to monitor their activities.

All those involved in the schemes were aware of the fines and the possible imprisonment they faced if caught; the lure of riches and the likelihood of little jail time kept them going. Public opinion also played a part in the continuing fraud. The social harm caused by white-collar criminals, especially those with high social status, was not known to the average person in the 1980s. It was commonly seen as a lesser evil than crime involving physical violence and injury. This opinion, however, was about to change.

The symbol of greed

In 1985 the SEC began an investigation after detecting suspicious activity on the stock market. With insiders trading privileged information, various company stocks were being purchased in a dramatic fashion just before a major announcement about a merger or sale of the company was made. The Southern District of New York also conducted an investigation at the same time as the SEC. The prosecutor in charge of the case was U.S. attorney and future mayor of New York City Rudolph "Rudy" Giuliani (1944–).

In 1986 the SEC investigation trail led to Dennis Levine. As a result, Levine made a deal with authorities and turned in his partner, Ivan Boesky. With solid evidence that Boesky was trading insider information, he entered a guilty plea on November 14, 1986. Boesky struck a bargain with Giuliani and the SEC that included a $100 million fine and a three-year prison sentence, served mostly at California's Lompoc Federal Prison Camp. As part of the deal, Boesky agreed to act as a government informer to help break up the illegal activities of others on Wall Street.

Because of Boesky's cooperation, subpoenas (court orders requiring testimony in court) were issued to some of America's wealthiest financiers, including Michael Milken. Boesky himself went from being one of the wealthiest and most successful figures on Wall Street to being banned from the securities industry. His name would forever be linked with scandal and corruption. Following his prison time Boesky continued living on his great wealth but avoided public attention.

Many saw Boesky as the visible symbol of the greed and excess of the 1980s. Oliver Stone directed a movie called *Wall Street,* inspired by the financial crimes of the decade. The script's main character was a high-powered financier who steals a line from Ivan Boesky himself when he announces that "greed is good."

For More Information

Books

Boesky, Ivan F. *Merger Mania: Arbitrage, Wall Street's Best Kept Money-Making Secret.* New York: Holt, Rinehart and Winston, 1985.

Bruck, Connie. *The Predators' Ball.* New York: Penguin Books, 1989.

Stein, Benjamin J. *A License to Steal: The Untold Story of Michael Milken and the Conspiracy to Bilk the Nation.* New York: Simon & Schuster, 1992.

Stewart, James B. *Den of Thieves.* New York: Simon & Schuster, 1991.

Web Sites

Cramer, James J. "Bad Boys, Bad Boys." *New York Magazine & Metro TV,* October 20, 2003. http://newyorkmetro.com/nymetro/news/bizfinance/columns/bottomline/n_9352 (accessed on August 15, 2004).

"Ivan-owe." Philadelphia City Paper. http://citypaper.net/article/112201/news.ivan.shtml (accessed on August 15, 2004).

"Moyers on Enron and History." *Public Affairs Television.* http://www.pbs.org/now/commentary/moyers.html (accessed on August 15, 2004).

Lizzie Borden

Born July 19, 1860 (Fall River, Massachusetts)
Died June 2, 1927 (Fall River, Massachusetts)

Accused murderer

"Lizzie Borden took an axe,
And gave her mother forty whacks.
When she saw what she had done,
She gave her father forty-one."

A children's rhyme

Lizzie Borden was accused in the gruesome double homicide of her father and stepmother in 1892. The violent nature of the murders and the gender of the accused killer made the case a national sensation. The trial had all the elements of a media drama, ensuring the high profile case a place in American legal legend and folklore. Most people in the late nineteenth century could not accept that a woman from a socially prominent family might be capable of such a crime. The matter was settled in the court of public opinion long before it ever went to trial. Numerous books, plays, and movies have been devoted to the murders. More than a century after the Borden trial, the case remains one of the most notorious in American history.

Fall River home

Lizbeth Andrew "Lizzie" Borden was born in 1860 to Sarah Anthony Morse and Andrew Jackson Borden, a decade after her sister Emma. Lizzie's mother died when Lizzie was two years old and her father married Abby Durfee Gray two years later. The family lived in a house on 92 Second Street in Fall

24

Lizzie Borden. *(AP/Wide World Photos)*

River, Massachusetts. Fall River was a country town that had grown into an industrial city by the 1890s.

Lizzie's father had started his career as a fish peddler but worked his way up in the community until he was a successful businessman and landlord. Although wealthy, Andrew Borden kept the modest house on Second Street he had purchased with his first wife. He did not even add the modern comforts of plumbing and electric or gas lighting as they became available. Originally built as a two family home, the narrow two and a half story house used two sets of stairs to get to the upstairs bedrooms. The Bordens used stairs off the kitchen and

Lizzie, Emma, and any guests used stairs off the front entrance. After a daytime robbery of jewelry and cash, her stepmother and father suspected Lizzie, who had a history of shoplifting. They installed a series of locks and bars throughout the house. By the time Lizzie was in her early twenties, the tension between the girls and their stepmother had grown. The addition of further locks separated both home and family.

Family tragedy

On August 4, 1892, Lizzie's uncle, John Morse, was in Fall River on business and he and Lizzie's father left the house early that morning. Lizzie's stepmother Abby was cleaning the second-floor guest room at around nine-thirty in the morning when she was struck from behind with a sharp instrument. The weapon, most likely a hatchet, hit her head and back nineteen times in all.

Andrew returned home over an hour later, found the doors locked from within, and rang the doorbell impatiently. Bridget "Maggie" Sullivan, the family maid, rushed to unbolt the door and let him in. Lizzie descended the stairs by the front entrance and greeted her father, telling him Abby had received a message and was not at home.

Andrew took the kitchen stairs to his bedroom before returning to the living room for his customary noon nap on the sofa. Minutes later the same weapon used on Abby delivered nearly a dozen blows to the man's face. Lizzie found her father and screamed for Maggie to come help. She then sent Maggie across the street to get family friend and physician Dr. Seabury Bowen.

When Dr. Bowen arrived, he confirmed Andrew Borden was dead and noted there had been no sign of a struggle. When the question of informing Mrs. Borden of the murder was raised, Lizzie said she thought she had heard Abby come in earlier. A check of the house revealed Abby's body upstairs and the police were notified of both murders.

A good daughter

Within a week it became evident that Lizzie Borden was a suspect in the murder of her father and stepmother. An inquest was held in which Lizzie contradicted herself and other

The couch where Andrew Borden was found murdered on August 4, 1892, displayed at the Lizzie Borden Bed and Breakfast in Massachusetts. In a nationally sensational trial, Lizzie Borden was acquitted of the murder of both her father and stepmother. *(AP/Wide World Photos)*

witnesses repeatedly. The town began to gossip about the family's problems, which were confirmed by a statement from Andrew's sister and brother-in-law, the Harringtons. They said money was a key issue of bitterness within the family. They believed intense jealousy was created when the usually stingy Andrew Borden gave gifts of property to Abby's family.

Lizzie was arrested on August 11 and entered a plea of not guilty the next day. When a preliminary hearing was held on August 22 the judge ruled probable cause existed to try Lizzie for murder. In November her case went before the Bristol County grand jury (a panel of citizens who determine if enough evidence exists to warrant a trial), who voted to in-

William H. Moody

William H. Moody (1853–1917) graduated from Harvard College in 1876 and was admitted to the Massachusetts bar in 1878. He practiced law in Haverhill, Massachusetts, and soon became interested in politics. Moody was appointed U.S. district attorney for the state's Eastern District in 1890. This led to his being a part of the team prosecuting the high profile Lizzie Borden murder case in 1893. Although Borden was acquitted, Moody's courtroom skills were recognized by leading Republicans of the day. He eventually served in Congress and the cabinet before being elevated to the U.S. Supreme Court as an associate justice.

William H. Moody. *(The Library of Congress)*

President Theodore Roosevelt (1858–1919; served 1901–09) named Moody secretary of the navy in 1902. In this position he was responsible for the build up and readiness of the naval fleet. In 1904 Moody was appointed U.S. attorney general, where he became one of Roosevelt's closest advisors on domestic issues.

In 1906 Roosevelt nominated Moody to the Supreme Court of the United States, and Moody was sworn in on December 17, 1906. He developed a crippling form of rheumatism (disease affecting muscles, nerves, and joints) and was forced to retire from the Court four years later after a full life of public service.

dict (formally charge a person suspected of committing a crime) and Lizzie was formally charged with murder on December 2, 1892.

The Borden trial was the media sensation of the year when it began June 5, 1893, at the New Bedford Court House in Massachusetts. Newspaper coverage surpassed that given to the Chicago World's Fair, which was going on at the same time. Most newspapers thought Lizzie was innocent and they publicly condemned the judicial system for putting her through such an ordeal after suffering such a personal loss.

The town of Fall River, however, was divided. Those in Lizzie's social circle defended her innocence while many in the working class were convinced of her guilt. George D. Robinson, a popular former Massachusetts governor who had served three terms in the state capital, headed Lizzie's defense team. The prosecutorial team was impressive and included the district attorney for the state's Eastern District, William H. Moody (see sidebar).

Her day in court

Moody gave a persuasive opening argument. He emphasized the resentments inside the Borden home as well as the vast inheritance Lizzie and Emma stood to gain. He noted motive and opportunity and stressed the absence of forced entry or burglary in the tightly secured home. Moody questioned Lizzie's alibi of being alone in the barn for the crucial few minutes when Andrew was attacked.

The other suspects considered in the case had other people to verify their whereabouts. Since Abby had died more than an hour before Andrew, Lizzie's story about Abby's leaving and returning home seemed to be a blatant lie. The state's case was strengthened when it was discovered Lizzie had destroyed the dress she was wearing the day of the murders. She was seen burning the dress in the kitchen wood stove three days later, claiming it was covered with paint. Also, witnesses testified that the day before the murders Lizzie visited a drug store in Fall River, where she attempted to purchase a poison, prussic acid. She explained that she needed the acid to clean a sealskin cape. The druggist refused to sell the prussic acid. Dr. Bowen, who had been called to the house August 3, said Abby and Andrew complained of stomach sickness and Abby suggested they had been poisoned.

The defense team managed to get Lizzie's contradictory testimony to investigators excluded from the trial. Her attorneys pointed to a lack of blood evidence and to Lizzie's prominent position in the community. They also succeeded in excluding testimony that Lizzie had tried to purchase a deadly poison the day before the murders.

The defense was helped by contradictory testimony about the murder weapon, and the media continued its favorable press toward Lizzie. The defense and the media both stressed that a murder this brutal and violent could not have been done by a gentle lady such as Lizzie. One day in court even, during discussion of the brutality of the murders, Lizzie fainted—the defense said due to her frail nature. When the jury went to deliberations on June 20 little doubt existed as to what the outcome would be. Massachusetts law at the time said that premeditated murder was a capital offense, condemning the offender to the gallows for hanging. The jury met for one hour before returning with a not guilty verdict.

American folklore

The courtroom erupted in wild cheering and thousands of well-wishers gathered to congratulate Lizzie on her acquittal. She soon took advantage of her newfound wealth to travel. She and Emma purchased a new home they called "Maplecroft." Not long after the trial, doubt began to grow in Fall River. People questioned whether Lizzie, now going by Lizbeth, had gotten away with murder.

By 1915 she was totally shunned by her community and estranged from her sister Emma, her most loyal defender. Lizzie Borden died in 1927 at the age of sixty-seven, from complications of pneumonia. She was buried, at her request, next to her father in the family plot at Oak Grove Cemetery in Fall River.

For More Information

Books

Hixson, Walter L. *Murder, Culture and Injustice: Four Sensational Cases in American History.* Akron, OH: The University of Akron Press, 2001.

Porter, Edwin H. *The Fall River Tragedy: A History of the Borden Murders.* Portland, ME: King Philip Publishing Company, 1985.

The Supreme Court of the United States: Its Beginnings and Its Justices—1790–1991. Washington, DC: Commission on the Bicentennial of the United States Constitution, 1992.

Web Site

"The Trial of Lizzie Borden: A Chronology." *University of Missouri.* http://www.law.umkc.edu/faculty/projects/ftrials/LizzieBorden/bordenchrono.html (accessed on August 15, 2004).

Ted Bundy

Born November 24, 1946 (Burlington, Vermont)
Died January 24, 1989 (Starke, Florida)

Serial murderer

Ted Bundy did not fit the stereotype of a murderer yet he was responsible for one of the most gruesome and notorious killing sprees in American history. Bundy was handsome and charming and lured dozens of unsuspecting women to their deaths. The sheer volume of those killed (suspected to be over one hundred) along with the random nature in which his victims were chosen made his case infamous.

The Ted Bundy case changed the way law enforcement handled homicide investigations. The case introduced the computer as an instrument of serial murder detection. It was used to organize large volumes of information as Bundy's crimes spread over several state lines. By the time he was apprehended, two dozen police agencies in four states were searching for Bundy. Despite the increased sophistication of information, many of the agencies were still largely unaware that they were pursuing the same individual.

Critical beginnings

Ted Bundy was born Theodore Robert Cowell at the Elizabeth Lund Home for Unwed Mothers in Burlington, Ver-

> "We serial killers are your sons, we are your husbands, we are everywhere. And there will be more of your children dead tomorrow."

Ted Bundy. *(AP/Wide World Photos)*

mont. For the first four years of his life he lived happily in Philadelphia, Pennsylvania, with his mother, Louise Cowell, and his grandparents. His mother then moved to Tacoma, Washington, where she met and married John Culpepper Bundy, known as Johnnie. Ted was soon joined by two brothers and a sister. Ted and his stepfather did not have a close relationship. By high school Ted referred to him as John.

Ted enjoyed skiing and the structured environment of the classroom where he felt confident. The opinions of the few friends he had were extremely important to him. He was regarded by his peers as scholarly. Most people at Wilson High School predicted he had a bright future when he graduated in 1965. But Ted was shy. By his first year at the University of Puget Sound, his high school friends had moved on and he was spending most of his time alone.

Ted's prized possession was a vehicle, a 1958 Volkswagen Bug he had purchased for $400. Ted transferred to the University of Washington in Seattle for his sophomore year and had his first serious dating experience. The woman soon broke off the relationship with him due to his immaturity. Devastated, he immersed himself in university classes and Republican Party politics.

Political connections

Ted Bundy served on the Nelson Rockefeller (1908–1979) presidential campaign in 1968 and the successful reelection campaign of Washington governor Dan Evans. Bundy was appointed to the Seattle Crime Prevention Advisory Committee, and later became an assistant to Ross Davis, the chairman of the Washington State Republican Party.

Due to his lack of finances and his need to keep up appearances, Bundy stole things he needed from stores and homes. He also continued a childhood habit of peeping into women's windows and developed a strong appetite for violent pornography. In order to relax before engaging in theft or voyeurism, Bundy would consume large amounts of alcohol. About this time, he traded in his beloved VW bug for a newer light brown, 1968 model.

Bundy had matured into a handsome man with striking blue eyes who dressed impeccably. University theatrical arts classes taught him about acting and makeup. He acquired a false mustache and other accessories that allowed him to change his appearance at will. While working for a medical supply company Ted stole a variety of props, including plaster casting material, splints, slings, and crutches.

Bundy earned his bachelor's degree in psychology in 1972. He briefly attended the new University of Puget Sound Law School before transferring to the University of Utah's law school in the fall of 1974.

Violence in paradise

Beginning in early 1974, nine young women vanished from college campuses and recreation areas in Washington and Oregon. Another young woman was severely beaten in her bedroom but survived after several months in a coma. The women ranged in age from eighteen to twenty-two years old. Two of the women's bodies would never be found. The seven that were eventually recovered had been left to decompose in wooded areas around Seattle, Washington.

All of the women had been assaulted and either bludgeoned (beaten with an object) or strangled to death. The few leads that law enforcement had discovered pointed to a handsome man who drove a Volkswagen and introduced himself as "Ted." He requested some form of help from the women who became his victims. Witnesses said the man's leg was in a cast and he was on crutches or his arm was in a cast and sling. He was very polite and friendly in asking for assistance in some task he was unable to do because of his injury. Public hysteria reached near panic when it became apparent someone was killing young women in the Pacific Northwest.

Authorities in Seattle and surrounding King County formed a multiple agency investigative task force when it

The 1968 Volkswagen Bug owned by serial killer Ted Bundy. The few leads that law enforcement had discovered pointed to a handsome man who drove a Volkswagen and introduced himself as "Ted." *(AP/Wide World Photos)*

became evident a violent killer was on the loose. (The term "serial killer" had not yet been introduced into police investigations but would later be used to perfectly describe Bundy.) Police received hundreds of calls each day on the "Ted Hotline." People called and turned in acquaintances, strangers, boyfriends, and husbands if they were named Ted, owned a Volkswagen, or vaguely resembled the composite pictures in the media.

Ted Bundy's name was among the first "Teds" reported to the Seattle authorities. The investigating task force received his name from a University of Washington professor, a former coworker, and from one of his girlfriends. He was one of over three thousand possible suspects delivered to the authorities. But the murders in the Northwest suddenly ended in the fall of 1974.

On the move

Bundy arrived in Salt Lake City in September to attend the University of Utah Law School. He settled into the life of a graduate student near the mountains and canyons of Utah's

Known Victims of Ted Bundy

Washington
1 February 1974: Lynda Ann Healy, age 21
12 March 1974: Donna Gail Manson, 19
17 April 1974: Susan Elaine Rancourt, 18
1 June 1974: Brenda Carol Ball, 22
11 June 1974: Georgann Hawkins, 18
14 July 1974: Janice Ott, 23
14 July 1974: Denise Naslund, 19
2 August 1974: Carol Valenzuela, 20

Oregon
6 May 1974: Roberta Kathleen Parks, 22

Utah
2 October 1974: Nancy Wilcox, 16

18 October 1974: Melissa Smith, 17
31 October 1974: Laurie Aime, 17
8 November 1974: Debbie Kent, 17
1 July 1975: Nancy Baird, 21

Colorado
12 January 1975: Caryn Campbell, 23
15 March 1975: Julie Cunningham, 26
6 April 1975: Denise Oliverson, 25

Florida
15 January 1978: Margaret Bowman, 21
15 January 1978: Lisa Levy, 20
9 February 1978: Kimberly Diane Leach, 12

ski country. In October 1974 three young women disappeared from small towns outside Salt Lake City. Law enforcement received a break in the case on November 8 when Carol DaRonch, an attractive nineteen year old, escaped a kidnapping attempt from a mall in Salt Lake City. The man who attacked her was dressed as a police officer and had requested her assistance in solving a crime. He drove a VW bug and introduced himself as Officer Roseland of the Murray, Utah, police department.

While DaRonch described her attempted abduction at the local police station, another abduction was taking place just twenty miles north at a high school parking lot in Bountiful, Utah. The kidnapped teenage girl was never seen again. The murders, however, stopped temporarily in Utah. It seemed they had moved to Colorado.

Between January and April 1975, three women disappeared from ski areas in Colorado. One body was recovered near Aspen but the other two were never found. By July 1975, the focus was back on Utah when a woman disappeared from the town of Farmington. Utah authorities were thrust into a new investigative area of the crimes. They were once again faced with the absence of evidence or a body.

Beginning of the end

Ted Bundy was stopped for a traffic violation in a Salt Lake City suburb during the early morning hours of August 16. Officers discovered robbery gear in the Volkswagen and Bundy, caught in a series of lies, was arrested on suspicion of burglary. The Utah sheriff's office then notified the Seattle task force that they had Washington resident Theodore Robert Bundy in custody and had confiscated a pair of handcuffs, an ice pick, a crowbar, a pantyhose mask, and several lengths of rope from his car. Investigators immediately began working to determine if Bundy was their killer in the Washington cases.

Carol DaRonch and several other witnesses picked Bundy out of a police line up. He was sent to trial on February 23, 1976. On March 1 the judge pronounced Bundy guilty of aggravated kidnapping, a first-degree felony, and sentenced him to one-to-fifteen years in Utah State Prison. He would be eligible for parole in less than three years.

Investigators in Washington, Utah, and Colorado continued their efforts to link Bundy to the homicides in their states. Evidence was mounting. By October 1976 officials presented Bundy with a warrant charging him in one of the Colorado murders. He was extradited (taken to the jurisdiction or area where a crime is originally committed) to Glenwood Springs, Colorado for trial. Bundy escaped in June 1977 during a pretrial hearing but was recaptured eight days later. He managed to escape again in December and this time he made it to Florida.

Life on the run

In January 1978 Bundy settled in Tallahassee, Florida, and began living his life as a fugitive under the alias Chris M. Hagen. By January 15, two women were dead and two more had been severely beaten in Tallahassee at Florida State University's Chi Omega sorority house, only a few blocks from Bundy's rooming house. On February 9 twelve-year-old Kimberly Leach was kidnapped from her Lake City, Florida, junior high school and brutally murdered.

Margaret Bowman and Lisa Levy. In 1979 Ted Bundy was convicted and sentenced to die in the electric chair for the murders of these two women. *(© Bettmann/Corbis)*

Bundy was arrested in January as he drove a stolen vehicle towards Pensacola, Florida. By this time sufficient evidence and eyewitness accounts existed to indict Bundy for the Tallahassee and the Lake City killings. In June 1979 a sensational trial, the first on national television, took place in Miami, Florida. Bundy was convicted and sentenced to die in the electric chair for the sorority house murders of Margaret Bowman and Lisa Levy. In Orlando, Florida, the following year Bundy was handed his third death sentence, this time for the murder of twelve-year old Kimberly Leach.

Bundy spent the next nine years on death row in Florida, filing appeals and giving select interviews. He ultimately confessed to thirty murders but estimates put the count as high as one hundred. He was never tried for most of his crimes. Bundy made a last effort to trade information on an additional fifty murders of which he had knowledge in exchange for a stay (delay) of execution. His appeals exhausted, Bundy was electrocuted on January 24, 1989, at the Florida State Prison in Starke.

For More Information

Books

Dobson, James C. *Life on the Edge.* Nashville, TN: Word Pub., 2000.

Garraty, John A., and Mark C. Carnes, eds. *American National Biography.* New York: Oxford University Press, 1999.

Michaud, Stephen G., and Hugh Aynesworth. *The Only Living Witness.* New York: Simon & Schuster, 1983.

Michaud, Stephen G., and Hugh Aynesworth. *Ted Bundy: Conversations With a Killer.* Irving, TX: Authorlink Press, 2000.

Rule, Ann. *The Stranger Beside Me.* New York: Norton, 2000.

Web Site

"Ted Bundy." *BBC News Online.* http://www.bbc.co.uk/crime/caseclosed/tedbundy1.shtml (accessed on August 15, 2004).

Truman Capote

Born September 30, 1924 (New Orleans, Louisiana)
Died August 25, 1984 (Los Angeles, California)

Author

Truman Capote was an author who became famous as much for his eccentric personality as for his writing. Capote initially wrote dark, mystical fiction but later shifted toward nonfiction. He preferred writing more about people and places than about issues or ideas. Capote's professional reputation was established when he helped create a new literary form known as the nonfiction novel in 1966 with his book *In Cold Blood* about the brutal murder of a Kansas family. It is a style of writing that combines literature, with its creative license, and journalism, which adheres to the facts.

"We will never know the reasons for what eventually happened, why he did what he did, but I still hurt thinking of it. It was such a waste."

Persons to Capote

Truman Capote was born Truman Streckfus Persons on September 30, 1924, in New Orleans, Louisiana. His mother, Lillie Mae Faulk, and his father, Archulus Persons, had a stormy relationship finally divorcing in 1931. Lillie Mae left Truman with relatives in a rural Alabama town called Monroeville when he was almost six years old.

Surrounded by adults, Truman spent a great deal of time alone and began writing stories. Lillie Mae moved to New

Truman Capote. *(The Library of Congress)*

York and changed her name to Nina. In 1932 she married Joseph Garcia Capote, a wealthy Cuban American businessman. Truman went to New York to live with his mother and stepfather in 1935 when he was ten years old. Joseph adopted him that year and his name changed to Truman Garcia Capote.

Truman attended Episcopal Trinity School, a private boys' school in New York, for three years. He was not a good student and his parents switched him to St. John's Military Academy in Ossining for three months. When the family moved to Greenwich, Connecticut, Truman attended Greenwich

High School. There his English teacher, Catherine Wood, recognized his talent and encouraged his writing. He dropped out of school at seventeen but completed his senior year in 1942 after the family returned to New York. While finishing his diploma, Truman found a part-time job as a copy boy at the *New Yorker* magazine.

Breakfast at Tiffany's

After graduating, Capote moved back to Monroeville and began working on an autobiographical book called *Other Voices, Other Rooms*. During the three years he spent on the project, Capote continued to write and submit other stories for publication. They began to appear in magazines, winning him several prizes. Capote's literary career was assured in 1948 when Random House published *Other Voices, Other Rooms*.

The success of *Other Voices, Other Rooms* brought Capote invitations to the best parties, clubs, and restaurants by the time he was twenty-five years old. He loved celebrities and the life of the socially prominent. Capote used these experiences with his new circle of friends to write the novella *Breakfast at Tiffany's,* which was published in 1958. The book became an instant hit and was made into a highly successful Hollywood movie, starring Audrey Hepburn (1929–1993) as the main character, Holly Golightly.

Capote experimented as a playwright, essay journalist, and screenplay writer with varying degrees of success. He even wrote a book and the lyrics for a musical comedy called *House of Flowers* in 1954. With his fame came endless invitations to dinners, parties, and social engagements. He was always invited because he was witty, charming, and loved to gossip. During these years he enjoyed the glamour and travel, but he also developed an addiction to alcohol and drugs. They would eventually take their toll on his health and his work.

In Cold Blood

Capote had been researching the topic of his next book when he came across a headline in the *New York Times* in 1959. A wealthy and prominent rancher, his wife, and teenage son and daughter had been brutally murdered in Holcomb, a suburb of Garden City, Kansas. Capote made arrangements to

True Crime

Ever since there have been criminals, there has been public interest in their crimes. People want to know why other people behave as they do, especially when it involves murder. There is widespread interest in what motivates killers to act, as well as curiosity about the details of what happens to the victims. The public will follow a case from the initial investigation by law enforcement officials, to the resulting trial and ultimate sentencing of the accused.

In the early twenty-first century, several television programs feature reenactments of actual criminal cases that have been solved. On these shows participating law enforce-ment officials and survivors are interviewed to show how criminals are brought to justice. Some programs give details of un-solved cases, asking viewers for help in apprehending offenders, while other televi-sion programs present fictionalized ac-counts of how modern technology is used in real crime scene investigations, especially for homicides.

Internet web sites and daily newspaper accounts follow current cases of true crime that capture the public's attention because they are either close to home or sensa-tional in nature. During the 1990s, media coverage of the latest killing by a celebrity,

do a series on the murders for the *New Yorker* and within days had moved to Kansas to write his book.

The result of Capote's investigation was *In Cold Blood,* a new type of novel involving true crime (see sidebar). Capote divided the book into four sections, moving the narrative back and forth between the criminals and their victims, and then between the detectives and the criminals. Capote used film techniques of flashbacks and close-ups to create maximum tension in the novel.

In Cold Blood was first serialized in the *New Yorker* and then released in book form by Random House in 1965. It sold out and created quite a sensation before being produced as a Hol-lywood movie in 1967. Capote celebrated his success by throwing a party at New York's Plaza Hotel in 1966, inviting five hundred friends to attend.

For several years after *In Cold Blood* was released, Truman was seen as an authority on the criminal justice system. Jour-nalists sought his opinion on prisons and capital punishment.

or one that was especially gruesome, created such public interest that a new type of book emerged. These written accounts give instant gratification to people who want to read about existing true crimes, but are often published before trial results are even in.

In 1965 Truman Capote helped introduce a new style of writing, which is now called "literary nonfiction." His novel, *In Cold Blood,* was based on facts, but he did not deliver them in a journalistic fashion. Instead he used a storytelling technique that made the book read like suspense fiction. Capote spent six years studying the 1959 murder of the Clutter family of Holcomb, Kansas. He lived with the townspeople, interviewing them over the years, while he recorded how they coped with the loss of four members of their community.

Capote maintained the suspense of his story by first talking about the community's response to the murders. He kept the details about how the Clutters died until after the killers were captured. Capote interviewed the two young drifters who confessed and were tried for the murders. He devoted the final chapter of his book to giving extensive details about their trial and prison life. Capote developed an emotional attachment to the criminals during his time interviewing them, and he witnessed their hanging at the Kansas state penitentiary in April 1965. Capote's in-depth novel was a great success and the popularity of true crime stories increased as a result.

In 1976 he wrote *Then It All Came Down,* which also dealt with crime and criminal justice.

Fall from grace

Capote earned large advances for his next project, a book and movie deal of a projected novel called *Answered Prayers.* The book was supposed to be a gossipy account of his jet-setting lifestyle and the famous people he knew. The first few chapters caused quite a scandal when they appeared in a 1975 copy of *Esquire* magazine. Capote was socially shunned by many of his former friends and acquaintances and the book was never finished.

The alienation sent Capote into a downward spiral of drug and alcohol abuse that lasted throughout the late 1970s and early 1980s. His substance abuse problems affected his writing but Capote continued to make the rounds on television talk shows. His flamboyant personality was still considered a novelty in the entertainment business. He even made a cameo

The tombstones for killers Richard Hickcock and Perry Smith, in the Kansas Museum of History. Executed in 1965, the two men were buried beneath the tombstones donated by author Truman Capote. Their murders of the Herbert Clutter family in Holcomb six years earlier were immortalized by Capote in his novel, *In Cold Blood*. *(AP/Wide World Photos)*

appearance in the murder mystery movie *Murder By Death* (1976). In 1977, he gave a reading of his works at a Maryland booking, but became so incoherent he had to be led off the stage.

After suffering from hallucinations and blackouts, Capote tried Alcoholics Anonymous (AA) and rehabilitation hospitals but always went back to his old habits. Shortly before his sixtieth birthday, Capote arranged to spend several weeks in Los Angeles with his friend and longtime supporter Joanne Carson. He died at her home on August 25, 1984.

For More Information

Books

Capote, Truman. *In Cold Blood: A True Account of a Multiple Murder and Its Consequences.* New York: Random House, 1965.

Clarke, Gerald. *Capote: A Biography.* New York: Simon & Schuster, 1988.

Garson, Helen S. *Truman Capote.* New York: Frederick Ungar Publishing Company, 1980.

Moates, Marianne M. *A Bridge of Childhood: Truman Capote's Southern Years.* New York: Henry Holt and Company, Inc., 1989.

Web Site

"American Masters: Truman Capote." *Public Broadcasting Service.* http://www.pbs.org/wnet/americanmasters/database/capote_t.html (accessed on August 15, 2004).

Clarence Darrow

Born April 18, 1857 (Kinsman, Ohio)
Died March 13, 1938 (Chicago, Illinois)

Defense attorney

Clarence Darrow was an attorney who championed the fundamental principle that everyone is entitled to a fair trial in a court of law. He promoted radical political and social causes and secured his place in history by opposing governmental and religious limits on individual freedom. Darrow helped sway public opinion toward tolerance of organized labor with the right of working people to unionize.

A lifelong opponent of the death penalty, he was an active member of the Amnesty Association, an organization formed to seek death row pardons (release from prison or legal responsibility for a convicted offense) for inmates who had not yet been executed for capital crimes. The Clarence Darrow Death Penalty Defense College is part of the University of Michigan Law School in Ann Arbor in the early twenty-first century. The college teaches the skills needed for attorneys representing those who face the death penalty.

As a courtroom speaker, Darrow was one of the first to favor plain words over the rhetoric, or flowery speech, used by most lawyers of the time. His realist style of public speaking was widely imitated by attorneys who admired his innovative

"I am pleading for a time when hatred and cruelty will not control the hearts of men. When we can learn by reason and judgment and a understanding and faith that all life is worth saving, and that mercy is the highest attribute of man."

Clarence Darrow. *(The Library of Congress)*

techniques of selecting jurors, interrogating hostile witnesses, and making closing arguments. Darrow's presentation skills have rarely been equaled. Building his legal practice with high-paying criminal cases and high-visibility causes, he was America's most famous trial attorney of the 1920s.

Early life and law career

Clarence Seward Darrow was born in 1857 in the small, rural village of Kinsman, Ohio. Born just before the American Civil War (1861–65; war in the United States between the

Union [North], who was opposed to slavery, and the Confederacy [South], who was in favor of slavery), he was the fifth of eight children of Amirus and Emily Eddy Darrow. In the community where Clarence was raised, most people opposed slavery. The "underground railroad" (a secret system to help slaves escape from the South) ran directly through the area where the Darrow family lived. This early experience had a lifelong influence on Clarence and his career, making him sensitive to the problems of minorities and the oppressed.

The Darrows were hardworking but poor and Clarence attended local public schools. He went on to attend Allegheny College in Meadville, Pennsylvania, and then taught school for a short time. He studied at the University of Michigan Law School for one year and became a member of the Ohio bar (legal profession) in 1878 at the age of twenty-one. Darrow married Jessie Ohl in April 1880. The young couple moved ten miles from Kinsman to Andover, Ohio, where Clarence set up a law practice. The couple's only child, Paul Edward, was born in 1883.

Clarence and Jessie divorced in 1897 and Darrow married a journalist, Ruby Hammerstrom, in 1903. Ruby and Clarence had no children together but Darrow maintained a relationship with his son Paul throughout his life. Darrow did not like either of his given names and was not called Clarence or Seward in his adult life. Known to his friends simply as "Darrow," he was called "Dee" by his wife.

In Andover, Darrow gained a reputation as a public speaker but opportunities for law were limited. Darrow and Ruby moved to Ashtabula, Ohio, a railroad town and a Great Lakes port. In 1885 Darrow was elected to the part-time position of borough city solicitor (the chief law officer of the town). This position gave him financial security while also allowing him time to build his private practice.

During his time in Ashtabula, Darrow discovered the political writings of John Peter Altgeld (1847–1902), which would redefine his life both personally and professionally. Altgeld was a strong supporter of workers' rights and their efforts to gain better working conditions from big business. Altgeld was a superior court judge in Cook County, Illinois, who became Illinois governor in 1892. Altgeld eventually joined Darrow's law practice in 1896.

Clarence Darrow, leaning on table, during the Scopes trial, in which biology teacher John Scopes was prosecuted for teaching the theory of evolution. (© Bettmann/Corbis)

Defending organized labor in Chicago

In 1887 Darrow made the move from Ashtabula to Chicago. He struck up an immediate friendship with Altgeld who guided his new protégé's career until Darrow became the general attorney to the Chicago and Northwestern Railroad in 1891. Darrow resigned his railroad position in 1894 to defend Eugene V. Debs (1855–1926), a labor leader charged with crimes related to a strike against the Pullman Company.

The trial marked the beginning of a series of criminal cases in which Darrow defended organized labor throughout the United States. This phase of his career ended in 1911 when Darrow himself was prosecuted for jury tampering in a Los

Angeles, California, murder case. After two trials against him, the prosecution ended with a hung jury (a jury unable to reach a verdict). Though Darrow was not convicted, he was not acquitted either and his reputation was severely damaged. He never worked on behalf of organized labor again. He returned to Chicago with his finances in ruin, trying to make a living in criminal defense work and rebuild his law practice.

Recovering his reputation

Through hard work, Darrow improved his reputation and took on two of his most famous cases. Both trials ran at a fever pitch in public opinion and guaranteed his place in history as a defense attorney.

The first was the Leopold and Loeb murder trial in Chicago. Nathan Leopold and Richard Loeb were two eighteen-year-old college students from wealthy families who were charged with the murder of fourteen-year-old Bobby Franks. Darrow's summation (the final part of an argument) before the jury seemed as much an attempt to change public attitudes concerning the criminal justice system and the death penalty as it was an attempt to keep his clients from hanging. Darrow would save over one hundred accused murderers from execution throughout his career.

The second was the 1925 Scopes trial that debated academic freedom versus legislative control over public education (see sidebar). In the Scopes trial, Darrow defended a science teacher, John Scopes, who was charged with violating Tennessee's Anti-Evolution Law, which prohibited teaching the theory of evolution (theory introduced by Charles Darwin [1809–1882] that all life is related and has descended from a common ancestor) in the state's public schools.

Although Darrow often defended wealthy or privileged individuals, he is most remembered for defending those accused of crimes tied to their race or to their political beliefs, such as radical labor union leader William "Big Bill" Haywood. Darrow's beliefs were rooted in populism (representing the common person), not socialism (an economic and political system in which the government controls all production).

Darrow's emphasis on individualism (belief that the rights of individuals outweigh the needs of the state), however, often

The Scopes Trial

In 1925 John T. Scopes, a twenty-four-year-old general science teacher and part-time football coach, faced charges brought by the state of Tennessee for violating its Anti-Evolution Law. William Jennings Bryan (1860–1925) was a Tennessee politician who guided the law through the state's legislature. The 1925 law made teaching the theory of human evolution in the state's public schools a misdemeanor, punishable by a maximum penalty of $500.

Although retired, Bryan joined the prosecution team to support the state's authority to control public school curriculum in the famous Scopes Trial. Clarence Darrow led a team of nationally prominent attorneys to defend Scopes's right to academic freedom in the public school system.

The lawsuit originated in the town of Dayton, Tennessee, when a copy of a newspaper arrived at the local drugstore with an American Civil Liberties Union (ACLU) advertisement. The ACLU announced it was offering its services free of charge to anyone who was willing to challenge the new Tennessee anti-evolution statute. Town leaders, including the school superintendent, became convinced the publicity generated by a controversial trial might help their dwindling population, which had fallen from a high of three thousand to only eighteen hundred by 1925.

They decided to use Scopes as their test case. Two local Dayton attorneys, also friends of Scopes, agreed to prosecute. The ACLU was contacted and began their selection of a high-profile defense team for the case. The Scopes case was headline news all over America for months before it finally came to trial. Because of the controversy, public feelings ran high and the trial captured the nation's attention.

A thousand people jammed the sweltering Rhea County Courthouse on July 10,

put him at odds with government programs. The Federal Bureau of Investigation (FBI) kept a file on Darrow. A memorandum written on June 24, 1936, which can be found at the Department of Justice's Freedom of Information Act Web site, noted that Darrow was a fine example of how "unscrupulous [without moral integrity] criminal lawyers stimulate disrespect for law and influence crime conditions."

Critic of the New Deal

Increasingly skeptical of government power, Darrow concluded his public career as a critic of President Franklin De-

1925 for the first day of trial. Hundreds of reporters covered the eight-day event, which was broadcast live over the radio to millions of homes and filmed for newsreels. It was the first live radio broadcast from a trial courtroom.

A carnival atmosphere pervaded the town with street banners, lemonade stands, and even chimpanzees performing in a sideshow. The court itself was moved outside to a tent in the courthouse square. Two thousand people crowded in by the final day of proceedings. The highlight of the battle within the trial was the sparring between Bryan and Darrow, the two famous attorneys. Darrow had been trying to engage Bryan in a public debate over science and religion for years and welcomed the chance at the Scopes trial.

The climax of events came when Darrow cross-examined Bryan, his longtime foe, after he called him to the witness stand as an expert on religion. The dramatic cross-examination by Darrow led to a furious argument until the judge finally called a halt.

The court narrowed the legal issue to whether Scopes ever taught the theory that humans were descended from other species and not from Adam and Eve as written in the Bible. The defense agreed to this fact; they asked jurors for a conviction so they could appeal the law. The jury convicted Scopes and he was fined $100.00. William Jennings Bryan died five days after the trial ended.

Ruling in 1927, the Tennessee Supreme Court upheld the statute but overturned Scopes's conviction on a technicality and directed prosecutors not to retry him. The Scopes trial had a profound cultural impact despite its legal insignificance. It was the focus of a popular Hollywood movie *Inherit the Wind* (1960). In 1968 the U.S. Supreme Court, in *Epperson v. Arkansas,* declared antievolution statutes to be unconstitutional as well as in violation of the constitutional separation of church and state expressed in the First Amendment.

lano Roosevelt's (1882–1945; served 1933–45) federal government programs introduced during the 1930s. Roosevelt had campaigned for president in 1932 promising a "New Deal" for the American people. The New Deal offered an unprecedented number of reforms addressing the catastrophic effects of the Great Depression (1929–41; the period, following the stock market crash in 1929, of depressed world economies and high unemployment). Congress was passing bills to relieve poverty, reduce unemployment, and speed economic recovery.

Although retired from his law practice, Darrow made national headlines when he received a presidential appointment. He was chair on a commission to study and review the operation of the National Recovery Administration (NRA) in 1934. The NRA was designed to address unemployment by regulating the number of hours worked per week and banning child labor. Despite his declining health, Darrow accepted the position because of financial difficulties.

Final days

By the 1930s Darrow still ran a small law practice when the legal profession as a whole was moving more toward the establishment of larger firms. Even though other attorneys admired his innovative techniques, Darrow was known for being unwilling to collaborate with other lawyers. Darrow became an outdated figure, respected by younger generations who had no interest in actually adopting his theories.

In failing health, Darrow was unable to find a lawyer to carry on his legal practice. His final years were spent as an invalid. He died in the Chicago apartment he and Ruby had rented for over thirty years. Darrow's career and triumphs went on to inspire many articles, books, plays, and films.

For More Information

Books

Blake, Arthur. *The Scopes Trial: Defending the Right to Teach.* Brookfield, CT: Millbrook Press, 1994.

Hynd, Alan. *Defenders of the Damned.* New York: A. S. Barnes, 1960.

Gurko, Miriam. *Clarence Darrow.* New York: Crowell, 1965.

McWhirter, Darien A. *The Legal 100: A Ranking of the Individuals Who Have Most Influenced the Law.* Secaucus, NJ: Carol Publishing Group, 1998.

Tierney, Kevin. *Darrow: A Biography.* New York: Thomas Y. Crowell, Publishers, 1979.

Web Sites

"Clarence Darrow." *National Archives Learning Curve.* http://www.spartacus. schoolnet.co.uk/USAdarrow.htm (accessed on August 15, 2004).

"Clarence Seward Darrow." *University of Missouri Faculty: Famous Trials.* http://www.law.umkc.edu/faculty/projects/ftrials/darrow.htm (accessed on August 15, 2004).

Thomas E. Dewey

Born March 24, 1902 (Owosso, Michigan)
Died March 18, 1971 (Bal Harbor, Florida)

Criminal prosecutor, governor

Thomas E. Dewey was an attorney who became a national hero for his success in prosecuting organized crime in New York City. He later played a crucial role in moving the United States forward as a major world power following World War II (1939–45; war in which Great Britain, France, the Soviet Union, the United States, and their allied forces defeated Germany, Italy, and Japan). He revived the Republican Party (GOP) in the 1940s and twice ran as the GOP presidential nominee. Elected governor of New York State in 1942, Dewey served for three consecutive terms. His administration established the state university system in 1947 and took the lead in public health and transportation policies. Under Governor Dewey, New York was the first state in the nation to enact laws prohibiting racial or religious discrimination in employment and education.

> "It is our solemn duty . . . to show that government can have both a head and a heart, that it can be both progressive and solvent, that it can serve the people without becoming their master."

Pursuing a career in law

Thomas Edmund Dewey was the only child of Annie Louise Thomas and George Martin Dewey, Jr. The Deweys

Thomas E. Dewey. *(The Library of Congress)*

were active participants in the Republican Party. Tom's father was editor for the family-owned newspaper, the Owosso *Times*. When Tom was fifteen, the United States entered World War I (1914–18; war in which Great Britain, France, the United States, and their allies defeated Germany, Austria-Hungary, and their allies) and he found himself part of the Boys Working Reserve, a program for young men under draft age who volunteered to fill the vacant civilian jobs caused by soldiers leaving to fight in the war.

After Tom graduated from Central High School in Owosso he attended the University of Michigan, studying both music and law. After graduating in 1923, he went on to receive a law degree from Columbia Law School in 1925. Dewey stayed in New York to work for several Wall Street law firms. In 1928 Dewey married Frances Eileen Hutt. The couple had two sons, Thomas Edmund Jr. and John Martin Dewey.

Gangbusters

Dewey left Wall Street in 1931 to become the youngest person to hold the title of chief assistant U.S. attorney for the Southern District of New York. It was the oldest and largest of the nation's ninety-four legal divisions. Dewey temporarily became U.S. attorney in November 1933 until Democratic president Franklin Roosevelt (1892–1945; served 1933–45) filled the post a month later. During his years in the department, Dewey actively prosecuted New York's most powerful organized crime figures.

In the early 1930s, violence in the criminal underworld was increasing as new, younger leaders were challenging the authority of the older gangsters. The outlawing of liquor, called Prohibition, in the 1920s had opened up the profitable business of bootlegging (selling illegal liquor), which led to the dramatic growth of organized crime. With the end of Prohibition in 1933, competition over control of other potentially lucrative illegal activities grew intense. These activities included loan-sharking, stolen goods, and narcotics, among others. The media was filled daily with reports of bloody battles between crime families.

New York City mayor Fiorello La Guardia (1882–1947), newly elected in 1934, was determined to rid the city of gangsters. La Guardia instructed Dewey to investigate "Dutch Schultz," whose real name was Arthur Flegenheimer. Police believed Schultz was behind a large number of crimes, but Schultz was murdered in a gangland slaying before Dewey could bring him to trial.

Dewey obtained seventy-two convictions out of the seventy-three prosecutions of leading criminals during his years as Special Prosecutor. Dewey's greatest success came when he obtained a conviction against Charles "Lucky" Luciano, in 1936. Luciano was New York's most notorious Mafia figure. By 1937 Dewey's fame had spread and he was elected district attorney of New York County.

Dewey and Dutch

Thomas Dewey's career as a public prosecutor in criminal cases against New York gang leaders was not without its personal hazards. He had a regular morning routine of leaving his home with two bodyguards and would call his office while stopping at a drugstore. Not until 1940, a gangster revealed that Dewey had been targeted for assassination at this drugstore stop only five years earlier by mob leader Dutch Schultz.

Dutch Schultz was born in the Bronx, in August 1902, to immigrant German Jews. Growing up in the tougher parts of the Bronx, he entered a career in crime at a young age. Dutch was convicted of burglary at age seventeen and served time in prison. By the mid-1920s, out of prison, Dutch established ownership of various breweries and speakeasies (places for the sale of illegal alcohol) in the Bronx and parts of Manhattan, supplying illegal liquor to eager customers during Prohibition when the sale and distribution of alcohol was prohibited. Known for his brutal ruthlessness, he sometimes personally rode as a guard on his trucks delivering the liquor. His competitors grew to fear him.

After Schultz survived the mob wars in 1930, the U.S. attorney's office began a lengthy investigation of Schultz's and associate Irving Wexler's bootlegging operations. Schultz was indicted in January 1933 on tax evasion charges for not filing tax returns from 1929 to 1931. Facing a potentially lengthy prison term, Schultz went into hiding for the next two years. He became the FBI's "Public Enemy No. 1," a title that added extra agents to the case and introduced wider cooperation among agencies. While Schultz was in hiding, Dewey began prosecuting the Wexler case in November 1933. He soon gained a conviction result-

Beginnings of presidential politics

Dewey used his national reputation as a criminal prosecutor to launch a career in politics. He was the Republican Party candidate for Governor of New York in 1938 and won the position in 1942 at the age of forty. By 1944 Governor Dewey was already a strong contender when he became the Republican candidate for president against Roosevelt. With World War II raging in Europe and the Pacific, however, Dewey was the underdog, since the American public usually does not change presidents during times of crisis. Although he lost to Roosevelt, Dewey was reelected New York's governor in 1946 by the largest majority in the history of the state.

Arthur "Dutch Schultz" Flegenheimer. *(AP/Wide World Photos)*

Schultz finally turned himself in to authorities in November 1934. His tax evasion trial began in April 1935 and resulted in a hung jury. A second trial resulted in a not guilty verdict in August 1935. During this time, New York governor Herbert H. Lehman (1878–1963) appointed Dewey as special prosecutor for the state to tackle the organized crime problem once again.

After Schultz's acquittal, Dewey began building a new case against Schultz. When Schultz heard Dewey was after him again, he started making plans to assassinate Dewey. He had one gang hit man study Dewey's daily routines. The plan was to shoot Dewey one morning when he made his drugstore stop. When other gang leaders learned of the plot, however, they feared this would only increase legal pressure on the mob's activities. To protect Dewey, they had two gunmen kill Schultz and his three bodyguards in a Newark, New Jersey, restaurant on October 23, 1935.

ing in a ten-year prison term and $50,000 fine. Afterwards, Dewey returned to private law practice.

A narrow loss

In 1948 Dewey once again secured the Republican nomination and ran for president, this time against President Harry S. Truman (1884–1972; served 1945–53). Despite his efforts in ending World War II and guiding the United States and its allies into a new postwar period, Truman entered the 1948 presidential campaign as the underdog. After the war, the american economy was struggling and people expressed their displeasure by giving Truman a poor approval rating. Even Truman's wife, Bess, predicted he would lose by a landslide. Dewey and his running mate, California governor Earl Warren, led in all the opinion polls.

President-elect Harry S. Truman smiles, holding an early edition of the November 3, 1948, *Chicago Tribune,* which mistakenly declared Thomas Dewey the victor. Dewey lost in one of the greatest upsets in American political history. *(© Bettmann/Corbis)*

Truman, however, added a new twist to political campaigning with what became known as "whistle-stops," quick stopovers in cities and towns along the railroad lines. The stops turned out to be a huge and unexpected success. At each whistle-stop Truman would speak to the crowd from the back of the train. He spoke casually to people who now felt like they knew the president and his family personally. He also blasted Dewey and warned that the Republicans would turn America into a nation by the rich and for the rich. Truman's folksy campaign style soon drew cheers of "Give 'em hell Harry," which resounded at each whistle-stop.

While Truman ran an aggressive campaign, Dewey tried not to be controversial to maintain his seemingly comfortable lead. Days before the election the media still predicted a Thomas Dewey White House and several of his aides even bought houses in Washington, D.C., in anticipation of the move. Dewey lost in one of the greatest upsets in American political history.

Dewey conceded defeat on the morning of November 3, 1948, while several newspapers, who had rushed the night before to get the morning edition out on time, ran the headline "Dewey Defeats Truman." A smiling Truman was shown holding the *Chicago Tribune* newspaper as his victory was announced to the world. Dewey returned to New York again and his job as governor.

Continued public service

Dewey was reelected as governor of New York again in 1950 and continued to be active in the Republican Party on a national level. In 1952 he helped Dwight Eisenhower (1890–1969; served 1953–61) win both the Republican Party nomination and the presidential election. When Dewey's third term as governor of New York ended in 1955, he returned to private law practice. He wrote *Journey to the Far Pacific* in 1952, and *Thomas E. Dewey on the Two Party System* in 1966.

Dewey declined an offer of nomination as chief justice of the Supreme Court in 1968, since he was caring for his ailing wife. Frances Dewey died in 1970 and Thomas Dewey died the following year, just a week short of his sixty-ninth birthday.

For More Information

Books

Karabell, Zachary. *The Last Campaign: How Harry Truman Won the 1948 Election*. New York: Alfred A. Knopf, 2000.

Smith, Richard Norton. *Thomas E. Dewey and His Times*. New York: Simon & Schuster, 1982.

Stolbert, Mary M. *Fighting Organized Crime: Politics, Justice, and the Legacy of Thomas E. Dewey*. Boston, MA: Northeastern University Press, 1995.

Wells, John A., ed. *Thomas E. Dewey on the Two-Party System*. Garden City, NY: Doubleday & Company, Inc., 1966.

Web Sites

"Presidential Politics." *PBS Online.* http://www.pbs.org/wgbh/amex/truman/sfeature/sf_ppolitics.html (accessed on August 15, 2004).

"Thomas Dewey (1902–1971)." *Eleanor Roosevelt National Historic Site.* http://www.nps.gov/elro/glossary/dewey-thomas.htm (accessed on August 15, 2004).

"Thomas Dewey." *The National Archives Learning Curve.* http://www.spartacus.schoolnet.co.uk/USAdeweyT.htm (accessed on August 15, 2004).

Charles Dickens

Born February 7, 1812 (Portsmouth, England)
Died June 9, 1870 (Kent, England)

Social reformer, novelist

Charles Dickens is considered by many as the most important writer of his time and remained the most widely recognizable British author, after William Shakespeare (1564–1616), throughout the twentieth century. He ushered in an age of serious attention to novelists with his dynamic writing, detailing the Victorian era (a very conservative period of formality among upper classes) in which he lived. Dickens's imaginative characters gave him the platform he needed to address the social reforms he had championed for over thirty years.

Dickens worked toward political and educational reform within Britain and was involved internationally in the promotion of prison reform and opposition of capital punishment. His popularity with the general public never declined during his lifetime, and he was seen as an advocate for the poor man. When the Dickens Fellowship was founded in 1902, it focused on Dickens's goal of remedying existing social evils to help the poor, oppressed, and unfortunate.

Early life of poverty

On February 7, 1812, Charles John Huffam Dickens was the second of seven children born to Elizabeth Barrow Dick-

"I believe that very few men are capable of estimating the immense amount of torture and agony which this dreadful punishment [solitary confinement], prolonged for years, inflicts upon the sufferers."

Charles Dickens. *(The Library of Congress)*

ens and John Dickens. His elder sister Fanny proved to be his best friend and had a profound influence on Charles his entire life.

John Dickens was a clerk at the navy pay office of Portsmouth when Charles was born, but the growing family moved often due to John's frequent transfers. Charles began his education at William Giles's school in Chatham, Kent. When his father was transferred to London in 1822, the family once again packed up and moved on.

By 1824 John Dickens had fallen behind with his creditors. He was arrested and sent to debtors prison, often referred to simply as *The Marshalsea.* At age twelve Charles found work at Warren's Blacking Factory wrapping bottles of black shoe polish. Six months later an inheritance provided enough money for John to leave prison and Charles resumed his education at a nearby private school, Wellington House Academy. When his father again fell into financial difficulties in 1827, young Charles left the academy and found employment as a clerk for the law firm of Ellis and Blackmore. Although he disliked the work, Charles enjoyed what was to become a lifelong habit of walking the streets of London in the late night hours gathering characters to inhabit his stories.

Seeking to improve his lot in life, Charles learned shorthand (a system of rapid handwriting using symbols to represent words) and started working as a freelance reporter in 1828 at the age of sixteen. By 1831 he was working for the *Mirror of Parliament,* a newspaper that reported the daily proceedings of the British Parliament. This marked the beginning of his interest in social reform. Dickens also began contributing articles to the radical newspaper *True Sun.* Using his considerable knowledge of what went on in the House of Commons, he worked to promote parliamentary reform.

American Notes

Dickens's first story, "A Dinner at Popular Walk," was published in 1833 in the *Monthly Magazine,* using the pen name "Boz." He married Catherine Hogarth in April 1836, and by 1837 the first of their ten children was born. By 1840, Dickens was the most popular author in Britain. Novels such as *The Pickwick Papers* (1836–37) and *Oliver Twist* (c. 1838) were soon followed by *A Christmas Carol* (1843). His fame spread across the world. In January 1842 the thirty-year old Dickens and his wife Catherine set sail from Liverpool to begin a tour of America.

Landing in Boston, Dickens received a warm welcome but as a staunch abolitionist (one who opposes slavery) he soon upset his hosts by condemning slavery. His writings were considered public property and had been adapted, imitated, and stolen on both sides of the Atlantic. As a result Dickens received no financial gain from the immense sale of his novels in the United States.

Prison Reform

In the early 1830s, two main disciplinary systems influenced the field of penitentiaries. Both came from America and were often referred to as the Philadelphia and the Auburn systems. They were named after the famous prisons in Pennsylvania and New York that had popularized them.

Under the Philadelphia, or Separate System, prisoners occupied individual cells day and night. They were sometimes given instructional books or handcraft exercises to do, but mostly they were left to meditate on their crimes and the consequences. Food was pushed into the cell through hatches and the prisoner never saw or spoke with anyone except the officers and a few approved prison visitors. Exercise took place in separate, individual yards.

Under the less strict version of the Separate System, prisoners left their cells for instruction or exercise but had to wear masks or veils to prevent seeing or being seen by fellow prisoners. The idea was that eliminating knowledge of fellow prisoners would reduce corruption upon release back into society. Critics used the term "solitary confinement" to describe the system and labeled it cruel and unusual punishment, especially for those whose sentences were for years or decades.

Under New York's Silent System, prisoners were allowed to work together but under very strict supervision. They were forbidden to speak or otherwise communicate with one another. Ideally, they were to sleep in separate cells but often they continued to sleep in the old dormitories of institutions unwilling to pay to replace the buildings. Wardens were required to be with the prisoners night and day, watching for any infringement of the rules.

The advantage of the Silent System was that it was easier to adopt in existing institutions, although it needed a very large staff to enforce discipline. The Separate System required an expensive building project, but required a much smaller staff to operate it. The merits of the two systems were hotly debated, with one side in favor of reforming offenders versus the other side in favor of deterring crime with severe punishment.

He had come prepared to advocate for an international copyright agreement to protect British authors as well as encourage budding American novelists. His speeches on the subject met with little response and the general opinion was in favor of continuing the existing practice. By June, when Dickens set sail for England aboard the *George Washington,* the enthusiasm that had greeted him was not evident at his farewell.

A substantial reading audience existed in England for books about America. Dickens's publishers had sent him off with a contract to write about his American adventures and compare American institutions to British ones. Dickens had expected to find a model democratic society against which British failures could be measured and criticized.

During Dickens's visit, his reputation in criminal law and prison reform (see sidebar) gave him access to tour several modern American prisons. His tour included the world famous Eastern Penitentiary in Philadelphia called Cherry Hill on March 8, 1842. Opened in 1830, it had become the international showplace for prisoner isolation, called the Separate System. It was the favorite method of more advanced nations of the period. Dickens denounced the Separate System as intolerably cruel in *American Notes,* published in October 1842. He was convinced that the suffering the Separate System inflicted on its victims produced no better results than other systems and probably far more harm.

Dickens noted that justice was not necessarily dealt out fairly. Much depended on a person's physical and financial resources. The poor and uneducated were always at a disadvantage. Dickens claimed this inequality especially held true in the case of the death penalty. He contended that executions were cruel, inefficient, and unevenly administered. He called for the death penalty to be abolished, arguing that judicial mistakes happened and were irreversible if the victim is dead.

Dickens also speculated in his writings about the effect of capital punishment on all those involved. He claimed the horror of public executions brought ruin on the community and affected the entire nation. Dickens believed there was a horrible fascination with the death penalty, and that this fascination was as harmful as the death penalty itself.

Dickens also sharply criticized slavery in America, as well as condemned America's corrupt politics and slanderous (false statements that damage a person's reputation) press. Not surprisingly, his book produced a great deal of resentment in the United States.

Although an extremely successful novelist, Dickens maintained his interest in social reform. Searching for a way to make a difference, he invested some of his royalties in a new radical newspaper called *The Daily News.* The newspaper regularly advocated progress and improvement of education, civil and religious liberty, and equal rights legislation. The paper began publication January 21, 1846, with Dickens as its editor.

At the same time, Dickens began work on the novel *David Copperfield.* The novel contained an autobiographical element and vaulted Dickens to the top of the list of popular English authors. *The Daily News,* however, was not a commercial success and Dickens moved on in 1850 to edit the weekly magazine *Household Words.* He continued his interest in charitable enterprises, including free schools for inner-city children, a program to rehabilitate prostitutes, and a low-cost housing project. Dickens was a lifelong advocate of national schools, which were not approved by Parliament until after his death in 1870.

Final tour

When Dickens had a disagreement with his partners in *Household Words* in 1859, he closed the journal and replaced it with *All the Year Round* that April. The new journal still covered social issues but also offered general interest articles and stories. Two of his most important works—*A Tale of Two Cities* (1859) and *Great Expectations* (1860–61)—first appeared as serialized novels in the magazine.

Dickens's continued practice of political agitation also kept him in the public eye. His fame led to a new adventure as an entertainer, using his own writings in public readings. The readings became an important part of his work and were made necessary, in part, by heavy financial obligations. The demands were due to his ever increasing family as well as the purchase of his dream home, Gad's Hill Place, in Kent.

Dickens's first public reading occurred in April 1858. His readings were so popular that he received an invitation to return to America and perform. He sailed for Boston aboard the *Cuba* on November 9, 1867, and landed ten days later amid a shower of rockets and flares welcoming him back. Both America and Dickens had changed in twenty-five years. Old resentments were forgotten during his tour of sixteen eastern cities.

Dickens triumphed on the stage as well as at the box office, but the schedule he kept exacted a heavy toll on his

The cover of an edition of *A Tale of Two Cities* by Charles Dickens. Dickens's novels and imaginative characters gave him the platform he needed to address social reform issues, including criticism of the prison system and opposition to capital punishment.

health. Returning to England in April 1868, the tour continued, as did his work as editor and publisher of *All the Year Round*. On June 9, 1870, Dickens died and was buried in the Poet's Corner of Westminster Abbey in London on June 14. Only about a dozen of his closest friends and family attended his funeral.

For More Information

Books

Collins, Philip. *Dickens and Crime*. London: Macmillan & Company, Ltd., 1962.

Davis, Paul. *Charles Dickens A to Z: The Essential Reference to His Life and Work*. New York: Checkmark Books, 1998.

Dickens, Charles. *American Notes*. New York: Penguin Books, 2000.

Kaplan, Fred. *Dickens: A Biography*. New York: William Morrow & Company, Inc., 1988.

Stephen, Sir Leslie, and Sir Sidney Lee, eds. *The Dictionary of National Biography*. London: Oxford University Press, 1938.

Web Site

"Charles Dickens: Novelist." *The National Archives Learning Curve*. http://www.spartacus.schoolnet.co.uk/PRdickens.htm (accessed on August 15, 2004).

Felix Frankfurter

Born November 15, 1882 (Vienna, Austria)
Died February 22, 1965 (Washington, D.C.)

Supreme Court justice

Felix Frankfurter was one of America's more powerful people in the legal profession who sought increased protection for criminal defendants in the early twentieth century. As a Supreme Court justice, he was a major force behind the creation and validation of President Franklin Delano Roosevelt's (1892–1945; served 1933–45) New Deal legislation. The New Deal was a collection of federal programs created in the 1930s to assist those most affected by the economic hardships of the Great Depression (1929–41).

As a legal scholar, Frankfurter was keenly interested in politics, and as a political progressive (one who seeks social reform though government action) he looked to create new legal means of tackling problems. He worked to expand the concept of equal protection under the laws for all, including those in the criminal justice system. Serving on the U.S. Supreme Court from 1939 to 1962, he and his colleagues were on the bench throughout the difficult years of the 1950s as racial segregation was challenged in the courts and brought an end to racially segregated public schools in America.

"It is a fair summary of history to say that the safeguards of liberty have been forged in controversies involving not very nice people."

Felix Frankfurter. *(The Library of Congress)*

Coming to America

Felix Frankfurter was born in Vienna, Austria, in 1882. He was the third of six children born to Emma and Leopold Frankfurter. Leopold was an unsuccessful Jewish merchant and in 1893 he set sail for America to search for greater economic opportunity and to escape Vienna's rising anti-Semitism (prejudice against Jews).

Emma Frankfurter and her six children arrived at Ellis Island in New York one year later aboard the *Marsala*. Felix did not speak a word of English when he began school at PS25 (Public School 25) on Fifth Street in New York City at the age of twelve. Emma was the dominant influence in Felix's life and she encouraged him to succeed as a scholar. He was an eager student who eagerly read books on literature, politics, and history. Felix spent hours reading journals from all over the world as he showed an early interest in world affairs.

Felix thrived on learning and went to the Free Academy of New York, now called City College. There he completed a program combining part of high school and all of his college requirements. In 1902, at the age of nineteen, he graduated third in his class of 775. Felix had long known that he wanted to be an attorney. He attended Harvard Law School where he was at the top of his class all three years before graduating in 1906.

While at Harvard, the philosophy of Professor James Bradley Thayer (1831–1902) impressed Frankfurter and became the foundation of his own jurisprudence (theories in law). Thayer counseled that, as a general principle, the courts should defer to Congress and the state legislatures whenever possible since legislators were directly elected by the public to solve social issues.

Dissenting views

Frankfurter began private practice with a New York law firm. During his first year he was appointed Assistant U.S. Attorney for the Southern District of New York under Henry Stimson (1867–1950). From Stimson, Frankfurter learned the art of trial preparation, which stressed not only to prepare for your own case but for the opposition's case as well. With his fondness for details, Felix gathered large amounts of credible evidence to support his oral arguments in court. Analyzing legal problems from multiple perspectives became Frankfurter's specialty. Stimson also taught him how to coax reluctant colleagues toward his point of view, a talent he perfected over time. When Stimson was appointed Secretary of War in 1910, Frankfurter accompanied him to Washington, D.C., to work as legal counsel for the Bureau of Insular Affairs.

Frankfurter had an exuberant style and a meticulous legal mind as well as a great deal of confidence in his own abilities to bring about consensus in any situation. Using his personality and keen intellect, he formed close relationships with those in power and used flattery and praise on those he most wanted to please.

In 1914 Frankfurter accepted an appointment to the faculty of Harvard Law School as professor of administrative law. From 1916 until 1918 President Woodrow Wilson (1856–1924; served 1913–21) called on him to investigate a growing number of labor disputes. Because of his outspoken support of individual civil rights and the protection of defendants' rights in criminal trials, he was often viewed as a staunch liberal (believing in the natural goodness of human beings and favoring civil liberties, democratic reform, and social progress).

In 1920 Frankfurter was a founding member of the American Civil Liberties Union (ACLU). The organization was created in response to the Red Scare (the American government and public fear of communism and its perceived threat to American democracy that led to mass arrests of foreigners) following World War I (1914–18; war in which Great Britain, France, the United States, and their allies defeated Germany, Austria-Hungary, and their allies). Communism was seen as a serious threat to American democracy and greatly feared by the public. Government agents arrested large numbers of people and held them indefinitely because of their political beliefs. The ACLU worked to defend the civil rights guaranteed in state and federal constitutions for those detained by law enforcement.

The case of Sacco and Vanzetti

One criminal trial that symbolized Frankfurter's advocacy of reform in the criminal justice field was the Sacco-Vanzetti case. In April 1920, at the height of the Red Scare, a payroll clerk and guard were murdered and robbed in the small industrial town of South Braintree near Boston, Massachusetts. Three weeks later two Italian immigrants, Nicola Sacco and Bartolomeo Vanzetti, wandered into a trap set by police to capture the suspects.

Neither Sacco nor Vanzetti had a previous criminal record, but they were known to authorities for their support of local labor strikes, antiwar activities during World War I, and associations with other political radicals. Though not considered suspects at first, police found that the two were armed and carried politically radical literature. Suspicion grew as the two

Nicola Sacco, left, and Bartolomeo Vanzetti stood trial and were convicted of crimes they did not commit in one of the most notorious political trials in U.S. history. Frankfurter and other advocates of reform in the criminal justice system used this case as an example to support their reform efforts. *(© Bettmann/Corbis)*

did not answer questions directly about their current activities, perhaps trying to protect others.

Both Sacco and Vanzetti were taken into custody and eventually charged with the crimes. The resulting court case was one of the most notorious political trials in the United States during the twentieth century. Their defense attorney aggressively attacked the police for focusing primarily on the defendants' political activities and involvement in the Italian anarchist (opposing structured governments) movement, rather than on evidence pertaining to the robbery and murders. Considerable publicity from the trial caught international attention. After a long six-week trial, the jury found them guilty on July 14, 1921.

Numerous attempts to appeal the verdict based on potential flaws in the trial's proceedings and even possible con-

The Supreme Court of the United States

The U.S. Supreme Court is located in Washington, D.C. It is the highest court in the United States and has ultimate judicial authority to interpret and decide questions of both federal and state law. As a result of this authority, it has had some of the greatest impacts on the nation's criminal justice system. The Supreme Court is the only court required by the U.S. Constitution. All other federal courts are created by Congress with intentionally limited jurisdiction. The Supreme Court has original jurisdiction in suits between states but most of its work consists of reviewing appeals from state supreme courts or lower federal courts.

The justices of the Supreme Court are appointed for life by the president and confirmed by a majority vote of the Senate. As of 2004, nine justices sat on the Supreme Court with one being appointed chief justice and the remaining members designated as associate justices. The U.S. Constitution provides, in Article I, Section 3, that if a president is impeached (charged formally with misconduct in office), "the Chief Justice shall preside" over the Senate trial.

On September 24, 1789, the Judiciary Act became law. In addition to establishing the Supreme Court, the act divided the country into three circuits, and established three circuit courts: Eastern, Middle, and Southern. The act did not provide separate judgeships for the circuit courts but directed that each was to consist of two Supreme Court justices and one district judge.

The Judiciary Act also established thirteen district courts and judgeships, providing at least one district court for each state then in the Union. The district courts functioned as trial courts, while the circuit courts served as trial courts for certain kinds of cases but also heard appeals from the lower courts. The Supreme Court was the highest appellate court and had the jurisdiction to review all appeals from the lower courts.

The Supreme Court first met on February 2, 1790. Since they still had no cases on the docket, the justices spent the first session attending to administrative matters

fessions to the crime from others in custody were rejected. The case grew in notoriety. Demonstrations were held in the United States as well as Europe on Sacco and Vanzetti's behalf for a retrial. These efforts failed too and the two men were sentenced to death on April 8, 1927.

Frankfurter stepped forward to rally public support by claiming that justice had not been served. With pressure from Frankfurter and other influential people, the governor of Mass-

such as the adoption of Rules of the Court and the admission of attorneys to the Supreme Court bar. The Court was to define what would be law and to invalidate any legislative or executive act that would be contrary to the Constitution.

During the first decade of the Court, the justices devoted most of their time to organizing the federal judicial system and riding circuit, visiting a series of federal courts located around a particular geographic area to hear appeals of cases, to hear cases as trial and appellate judges. Civil disputes between citizens of different states as well as controversies concerning national government and its laws comprised most of the early cases heard. Previously there had only been state courts and the concept of the "United States" was relatively new, so many were initially reluctant to accept the new federal authority.

Although the circuit-riding of justices played an important role in educating citizens about their federal government, it took a heavy toll on those serving. Justices wrote to family and friends recounting the physical challenges of riding the circuit by horseback, stagecoach, and steamboat while lodging in taverns and public houses for long periods of time each year. Finally, in 1891, Congress passed the Circuit Court of Appeals Act establishing nine Circuit Courts of Appeals with permanent judgeships.

For the next 170 years, the Court issued few rulings related to rights of defendants or victims in the criminal justice system. The Court would make its mark in criminal law in the 1960s under the leadership of Justice Earl Warren (1891–1974). The Court made several landmark decisions between 1961 and 1966 affirming the rights of the accused in the criminal justice system from such police actions as illegal search and seizure (known as the exclusionary rule) and advising suspects of their rights before interrogations (Miranda rights).

The exclusionary rule states that evidence illegally obtained by the police cannot be used in a court of law. Miranda rights state that police must advise a person being arrested that they have the right to remain silent, that anything they say can be used against them in court, they have the right to have a lawyer, and that a lawyer will be provided if the person cannot afford one.

achusetts formed a committee that included the president of Harvard University. The committee was to determine if the governor should grant clemency (reduce the severity of the sentence) for the defendants. After a quick review, the committee determined clemency was not in order.

Sacco and Vanzetti were executed on April 23. Frankfurter protested what he claimed was the unjust nature of the entire case. He charged that the trial was driven by a strong bias against immigrants and political radicals. Decades later after several reviews, researchers could still not find sufficient evidence to support the guilt of either Sacco or Vanzetti.

A Harvard legal adviser

After a six-year courtship, Felix had married Marion Denman in 1920. The couple had no children together. Although he remained at Harvard, Frankfurter continued to exert his influence in Washington, D.C. When Franklin Delano Roosevelt (1892–1945; served 1933–45) became president, he often consulted Frankfurter, a fellow Democrat, about the legal implications of his New Deal legislation. As a result of this work, Frankfurter placed many of his Harvard students in important positions as law clerks in the new agencies Roosevelt created. These young people earned the name "the Happy Hot Dogs of Felix Frankfurter."

Supreme Court justice

When Roosevelt was given the opportunity to refill a number of the Supreme Court justice positions after a series of retirements, he nominated Frankfurter. Frankfurter was sworn in as an associate justice on January 30, 1939. Frankfurter's passion for the democratic process dominated his case deliberations. He dedicated his twenty-three years on the Supreme Court as a leading proponent of judicial restraint, meaning he believed the country's best hope for the protection of democratic values rested within the elected branches of government —the legislative and executive branches—not the judicial branch. (The legislative branch makes laws; the executive branch puts the laws into effect; and the judicial branch enforces the laws by administering justice.)

Frankfurter argued in favor of leaving it to the legislative branch to pass the nation's laws, which the courts would then interpret. This legal position angered and frustrated many of those who had initially been pleased with his appointment to the Supreme Court. Many wanted Frankfurter to be much more aggressive in expanding the constitutional safeguards for defendants in criminal cases, as he had during the Red Scare of the 1920s.

Nonetheless Frankfurter remained true to his earliest convictions of judicial restraint throughout his career. He retired from the Court on August 28, 1962, following a stroke. Felix Frankfurter died on February 22, 1965, at the age of eighty-two. The Supreme Court adopted many of his earlier beliefs concerning defendants' rights to fair trials after his death. The Court passed a series of rulings in the late 1960s greatly altering the criminal justice process.

For More Information

Books

McWhirter, Darien A. *The Legal 100: A Ranking of the Individuals Who Have Most Influenced the Law.* Secaucus, NJ: Citadel Press, 1998.

Simon, James F. *The Antagonists: Hugo Black, Felix Frankfurter and Civil Liberties in Modern America.* New York: Simon & Schuster, 1989.

The Supreme Court of the United States: Its Beginnings and Its Justices—1790–1991. Washington, DC: Commission on the Bicentennial of the United States Constitution, 1992.

Web Sites

"Biographies of Supreme Court of the United States Justices: Felix Frankfurter." *Wikipedia: The Free Encyclopedia.* http://en.wikipedia.org/wiki/United_States_Supreme_Court (accessed on August 15, 2004).

"Felix Frankfurter." *The National Archives Learning Curve.* http://www.spartacus.schoolnet.co.uk/USAfrankfurter.htm (accessed on February 20, 2004).

Emma Goldman

Born June 27, 1869 (Kovno, Russia)
Died May 14, 1940 (Toronto, Ontario, Canada)

Social activist

"The kind of patriotism that we represent is the kind which loves America with open eyes. . . . We love the dreamers and the philosophers and the thinkers who are giving America liberty. But that must not make us blind to the social faults of America."

Emma Goldman came to America and made a career of challenging the legitimacy of government, religion, and property. Throughout her political life she championed the constitutional right to freedom of speech and worked to improve conditions for the poor, laborers, and immigrants. Goldman criticized the social and economic subordination of women and was a lifelong opponent of war.

Goldman was an anarchist (person opposed to organized governments), so she rejected any enforced political order by an individual or government. She believed people were essentially good and that all forms of government authority were unnecessary and undesirable. She argued for a new social order based on the voluntary cooperation of individuals and groups.

Goldman reached beyond the predominantly ethnic, immigrant audience that typically constituted anarchists in the early parts of the twentieth century and helped make the radical movement more mainstream in America. Like many anarchists, Goldman proclaimed her mission as one of promoting critical thinking, cultural and political change, and

Emma Goldman. *(The Library of Congress)*

social cooperation based on personal liberty. Emma's political activities inspired criminal laws banning the practice of radical politics. She was also a frequent defendant in criminal cases involving her political activities.

A social commitment

In the summer of 1868 Abraham Goldman married Taube Zodokoff, a widow with two daughters. Emma Goldman was born to the couple a year later and was soon followed by two boys. Abraham was an innkeeper in the small Lithuanian town of Papile. Jewish citizens were in the majority but German culture was dominant. The Russian Tsar, the supreme ruler of Russia, held political power in the area. Since the family inn also served as a training center for the Russian military, the Goldman family directly felt the authority of the Russian government.

At the age of seven, Emma was sent to the Prussian seaport of Konigsberg to live with relatives and attend a private Jewish elementary school, despite her father's reluctance to have an educated daughter. Emma transferred to a public school when her family moved to Konigsberg. It was there that young Emma was befriended by a teacher who introduced her to opera and literature and encouraged her dreams.

When Emma was twelve her father moved the family once again, this time to the large city of St. Petersburg, Russia, to seek work. Emma's formal education ended there as she and her siblings were required to work to supplement the family income. Emma continued to educate herself with every opportunity in the sophisticated city of St. Petersburg, which was also home to a rising generation of Russian political radicals.

Emma became fascinated with female political martyrs (women who gave their lives for a political cause) and was influenced in particular by Nikolay Chernyshevsky's novel, *What is to Be Done?* In it, the heroine rejects her perceived destiny in order to become an ordinary physician among Russia's poor people.

With the collapse of the radical movement in Russia and facing pressure from her father to marry, young Emma decided she needed to leave Russia to pursue her dream of independence and social commitment. In 1885 at the age of sixteen, Emma arrived in the United States with her half-sister Helena aboard the German steamship *Elbe*. It was the same year that the Statue of Liberty was shipped to New York City from France to welcome immigrants such as Emma.

The girls lived with their elder sister Lena and found jobs in the expanding industrial city of Rochester, New York. Emma worked factory jobs and soon met a fellow laborer, Jacob Kersner, whom she married in 1886. Although the couple divorced in 1889, the marriage provided Emma with a claim to U.S. citizenship.

Emma Goldman stands on a car as she speaks at Union Square. A well-known anarchist and lecturer, Goldman fought to achieve a cooperative commonwealth in America and was often arrested by local officials on charges such as conspiracy and inciting a riot.
(© Bettmann/Corbis)

Radical activities

In 1886, Goldman closely followed the news of the Haymarket trials in Chicago, Illinois. Violence had erupted at an anarchist rally in Haymarket Square, resulting in the bombing deaths of seven policemen. Four anarchist labor leaders were convicted of conspiracy and executed, even though the actual bomber was never identified.

Goldman was deeply moved by the trial results. She joined the anarchist movement before moving to New York City in 1889 to participate in radical activities. She met her lifelong friend, Alexander Berkman (1870–1936), and helped him plot the assassination of industrialist Henry Clay Frick of the Carnegie Steel Company. It was a misguided effort to end the

Homestead Steel strike. Frick was merely wounded and, in 1892, Berkman was sentenced to fourteen years in prison. The event made Goldman infamous when the *New York World* newspaper portrayed her as the mastermind of the plot.

A national economic crisis set off by the failure of four major railroad companies hit America in "The Panic of 1893." The stock market crashed and hundreds of thousands of workers lost their jobs. New York City streets filled with the hungry and unemployed. The city's police, anxious to control the rising unrest, turned their attention to anarchists whose inflammatory speeches were aggravating an already tense situation.

By this time, Goldman was a well-known anarchist and lecturer who advocated for the poor. She addressed a public rally of some three thousand people at Union Square in August 1893 and was arrested for inciting a riot. While awaiting release on bail, Goldman was interviewed by the *World's* famous female reporter, Nellie Bly (c. 1867–1922).

As relayed in Brooke Kroeger's 1994 book *Nellie Bly: Daredevil, Reporter, Feminist* Bly wrote, "Do you need an introduction to Emma Goldman? . . . You have seen supposed pictures of her. You have read of her as a property-destroying, capitalist-killing, riot-promoting agitator." Bly then described the real Goldman as a "little bit of a girl, just five feet high, . . . not showing her one hundred twenty pounds; with a saucy, turned up nose and very expressive blue-gray eyes that gazed inquiringly at me through shell-rimmed glasses."

While most reporters of the day were unsympathetic, Bly described Goldman as neat, immaculate, and well-dressed. Where the *New York Times* referred to Goldman as a fire-eating anarchist, Bly dubbed her "the little anarchist, the modern Joan of Arc," in a highly sympathetic report to her newspaper.

New criminal laws

Upon her release from prison in 1895, Goldman went to Europe where she studied medicine before returning to the United States and continuing her radical activities. In 1901 she was implicated in the murder of President William McKinley (1843–1901; served 1897–1901). Goldman was released because no evidence could be gathered against her, other than that the assassin had attended one of her speeches.

McKinley's assassination led to the passage of the 1902 Aliens Act. The act declared the advocacy of "criminal anarchy" to be a felony. The law became the judicial basis for all future expulsions and deportations from America. Goldman, later dubbed "Red Emma" because of her radical politics associated with the rise of the Communist Party in Russia whose symbolic color was red, founded the Free Speech League in 1903 to promote the right to freedom of speech and freedom of assembly. She claimed the constitutional right for herself as well as other anarchists like Big Bill Haywood and his militant trade union (see sidebar).

From 1906 until 1917 Goldman edited and published the monthly journal *Mother Earth*. The magazine advocated the banning of all government and recommended it be replaced by voluntary cooperation among the people. She targeted all forms of repression—economic, political, and psychological. She worked in hopes of achieving a cooperative commonwealth in America. Goldman put her energies into lecturing, writing, and tireless political organizing. These activities led to her arrest in the spring of 1916. She received a fifteen-day prison term for giving a public lecture on birth control.

On June 15, 1917, officers arrived once again at the office of *Mother Earth* with a warrant for her arrest on charges of conspiracy to convince persons not to register for the draft. She and Alexander Berkman, who was arrested as well, each received a two-year prison sentence for their opposition to America's involvement in World War I (1914–18; war in which Great Britain, France, the United States, and their allies defeated Germany, Austria-Hungary, and their allies).

The federal government, led by a newly empowered J. Edgar Hoover (1895–1972) of the U.S. Justice Department, targeted Goldman for deportation as part of the "Palmer Raids" of 1919. The raids on aliens known or suspected of being political radicals resulted in thousands of arrests of mostly aliens (people with citizenship in other countries) believed to be political radicals in over thirty cities, but only around 250 were actually deported.

Hoover labeled Goldman the "Red Queen of Anarchy" and was waiting for her and Berkman upon their release from prison in Jefferson City, Missouri. Hoover needed a high profile case in his campaign against communists and subversives

William Haywood

William Dudley "Big Bill" Haywood (1869–1928) was a miner in Silver City, Idaho, when he became interested in the labor movement. In 1896 he joined the Western Federation of Miners (WFM) and became active in union campaigns to increase wages and end child labor in the mines. He progressed through the ranks of the national executive board until deciding that labor problems required more revolutionary solutions.

Haywood and his political friends joined together in 1905 to form the radical labor organization, Industrial Workers of the World (IWW). Known as "the Wobblies," they wanted to unify all labor and place production in the hands of the workers. The IWW advocated strikes, boycotts, and passive resistance by their members. They were also accused of using violence and sabotage.

In 1906 the WFM and its leaders including Haywood were brought to trial for the murder of former Idaho governor, Frank Steunenberg (1861–1905). Famous attorney **Clarence Darrow** (1857–1938; see entry) defended Haywood and several others and they were acquitted in 1907. The trial received enormous publicity for its dramatic details. It was the first trial to be covered by the press wire services.

Haywood soon left the WFM and devoted his time and energy to the Socialist Party of America (believes that both the economy and society should be run democratically in order to meet public needs, not to make profits for a few) and the IWW. He was recognized as the spokesperson for industrial workers and was celebrated by various nonworking class socialists who turned

(those who seek overthrow of a government). Hoover had arranged for the deportation of nearly two hundred and fifty anarchists aboard the *Buford*. Dubbed, the "Soviet Ark," the decrepit, old transport ship carried its human cargo out of the New York harbor bound for Russia with Emma Goldman as its most famous passenger.

Adrift

Goldman was at first sympathetic to the new Soviet Union and its communist government. She became disillusioned, however, after witnessing the blatant disregard of civil liberties by Vladimir Lenin's (1870–1924) revolutionary government led by the Communist Party that banned all private property giving the government total control of the economy.

William Haywood. *(The Library of Congress)*

him into a public personality. The *New York Times* called Haywood "the most hated and feared figure in America," for his role in labor organization.

The IWW opposed U.S. participation in World War I and Haywood produced antiwar propaganda when America entered the conflict in 1917. That September the Justice Department conducted raids on the IWW headquarters in twenty-four cities. They seized books, minutes of meetings, financial records, and membership lists. Haywood and others were arrested under the Espionage Act for conspiracy and interference with conscription (the military draft).

In 1918 he was convicted and sentenced to twenty years in prison and fined $10,000. While awaiting the result of an appeal for a new trial in 1921, Haywood jumped bail and fled to the Soviet Union. He died in Moscow in 1928.

By 1921 Emma fled the Soviet Union. She managed to obtain British citizenship by marrying a Welsh miner sympathetic to her plight. She spent the final two decades of her life traveling between England, Canada, and France, speaking out for her own humanist brand of anarchism.

Goldman wrote *My Disillusionment in Russia* in 1923 and published her autobiography, *Living My Life,* in 1931. By 1934 the political mood in the United States had changed as the fear of communism had declined. The aging Emma was allowed to return for a ninety day speaking tour. She lectured in sixteen cities, from New York to St. Louis. She spoke out against both German fascism (government marked by dictatorship, government control of the economy, and suppression of all opposition) and Soviet communism (government in which the state controls the economy and all property and wealth are shared equally by the people) to produce world opinion against them.

Goldman left the country as she had arrived, an anarchist and a radical who spoke on her own terms. Upon her death in 1940 at the age of seventy-one, the U.S. government granted permission for Goldman's body to be returned to the country for burial at Waldheim Cemetery in Chicago, Illinois.

For More Information

Books

Chalberg, John. *Emma Goldman: American Individualist.* New York: Longman, 1991.

Dubofsky, Melvyn. *"Big Bill" Haywood.* New York: St. Martin's Press, 1987.

Kroeger, Brooke. *Nellie Bly: Daredevil, Reporter, Feminist.* New York: Times Books, 1994.

Walker, Martin. *America Reborn: A Twentieth-Century Narrative in Twenty-Six Lives.* New York: Alfred A. Knopf, 2000.

Web Sites

"Emma Goldman." *Board of Regents of the University of Wisconsin System.* http://us.history.wisc.edu/hist102/bios/20.html (accessed on August 15, 2004).

"William Haywood." *The National Archives Learning Curve.* http://www.spartacus.schoolnet.co.uk/USAhaywood.htm (accessed on August 15, 2004).

J. Edgar Hoover

Born January 1, 1895 (Washington, D.C.)
Died May 2, 1972 (Washington, D.C.)

Director of the Federal Bureau of Investigation (FBI)

During his tenure J. Edgar Hoover built the Federal Bureau of Investigation (FBI) into one of the most powerful law enforcement agencies in the world. Appointed director in 1924, he held the position for nearly fifty years, through eight presidents beginning with Calvin Coolidge (1872–1933; served 1923–29) and ending with Richard Nixon (1913–1994; served 1969–74).

Though gaining great fame for his apprehension of several famous outlaws, Hoover's primary notoriety as the nation's leading law officer came from attacking potential criminal activity by political radicals over several decades. Hoover contributed to national stability and security during the intense international and domestic emergencies of the Bolshevik Revolution (takeover of Russia by communists), the Nazi threat of World War II (1939–45; war in which Great Britain, France, the Soviet Union, the United States, and their allied forces defeated Germany, Italy, and Japan) and the Cold War (1945–91). The Cold War was an intense political and economic rivalry from 1945 to 1991 between the United States and the Soviet Union falling just short of military con-

> "I have observed the rise of international communism with great concern, particularly communist efforts to infiltrate and infect our American way of life."

J. Edgar Hoover. *(National Archives and Records Administration)*

flict. Communism is a governmental system in which a single party controls all aspects of society. In economic theory, it bans private ownership of property and businesses so that goods produced and wealth accumulated are shared equally by all.

Hoover is also considered one of the leading innovators in American governmental history for his application of science and technology to police work. The FBI headquarters on Pennsylvania Avenue in Washington, D.C., is named the J. Edgar Hoover Building.

Born on Capitol Hill

John Edgar Hoover was born in Washington, D.C., on January 1, 1895. Annie Marie Scheitlin Hoover and Dickerson Naylor Hoover had four children and Edgar was the youngest. Everyone in the family, except his mother, called him J. E. The family lived at 413 Seward Square, a row house located behind the Library of Congress on Capitol Hill.

Dickerson, like his father before him, worked for the U.S. Coast and Geodetic Survey. He was chief of the printing division but was forced to resign in 1917 following a mental breakdown. Annie was the greatest influence on young Edgar. She held old-fashioned values and made sure her children did too. Edgar stuttered as a youth but overcame the problem when he read an article that said talking faster not slower would help, and it worked.

Edgar was frail and not athletic as a child, but he put his energy into areas where he knew he could excel. Working after school delivering groceries, he found the more trips he made the more tips he received. So he would work fast to make as much money as possible each day. That, along with his rapid speech, earned him the nickname "Speedy."

Edgar took up debate and by his junior year at Central High School led the debate team. Hoover found that if he could dominate a conversation he could control it, and that became his trademark. His main interest in high school was the school cadet corps where he moved quickly up through the ranks. By the start of his senior year, Edgar passed the ROTC officers' exam, was promoted to captain, and given command of Company B of the Central High School Cadet Regiment. In 1913 he led his unit in President Woodrow Wilson's (1856–1924; served 1913–21) first inaugural parade. Young Edgar was promoted to command Company A and served as valedictorian (one who graduates at the top of his or her class).

The Justice Department

Hoover worked at the Library of Congress for five years while attending night school at George Washington University. He received a law degree in 1916 and went on to earn a master's degree in law before passing the bar exam (a test to

The Palmer Raids

America was affected by a series of severe social conflicts following World War I. Skyrocketing prices, nationwide strikes, revolutions throughout much of Europe and signs of a serious threat from radicals at home created a sense that the nation was under attack. Passage of both Prohibition (Eighteenth Amendment, making alcohol illegal) and Women's Suffrage (Nineteenth Amendment giving women right to vote) in 1919 reflected a change in the national character.

The fear of communism and political conspiracies ran high, in a phenomenon called the "Red Scare" from the association of Soviet communism with the color red, later a prominent color of the Soviet Union's flag. The perceived threat of a communist menace escalated in 1919 with a series of bombings against leading politicians. Public outcry reached fever pitch on the evening of June 2, 1919, when a number of bombs were detonated within an hour of each other in eight eastern cities, including Washington, D.C. One bomb partially destroyed the home of newly appointed attorney general A. Mitchell Palmer (1872–1936).

With President Woodrow Wilson preoccupied with the World War I peace treaty and bedridden by strokes, the nation's problems fell under the jurisdiction of the attorney general. New to his position, Palmer depended on the advice of his employees. He assembled a new General Intelligence Division (GID) at the Department of Justice with responsibility for investigating the strength of radical political organizations in the United States.

determine suitability to practice law in a state) in 1917. In July of that year, three months after the United States entered World War I (1914–18), Hoover obtained a draft-exempt position with the Alien Enemy Bureau of the Department of Justice (DOJ). The DOJ would be his only employer in a Washington career exceeding fifty-five years.

With many of America's youth at war, the DOJ was understaffed and Hoover's rise was rapid. He was placed in charge of a unit in the Enemy Alien Registration Section and by 1919 was appointed chief of the new General Intelligence Division (GID). He was special assistant to attorney general and presidential hopeful A. Mitchell Palmer (1872–1936). At the age of twenty-four, Hoover was given responsibility for directing a newly formed section to gather evidence on revolutionary and politically radical groups.

Palmer recruited J. Edgar Hoover as his special assistant and appointed him chief of the GID. By the fall of 1919 Hoover reported that radicals posed a real threat to the U.S. government. He advised drastic action be taken against a possible revolution. Under intense pressure from Congress and the public, Palmer clamped down on political dissent and agreed to deport many alien (foreign) radicals. Because the peace treaty had not yet been signed, Palmer decided that he could make use of extraordinary wartime powers under the Sedition Act of 1918 and the Espionage Act of 1917.

These acts made it a crime to interfere with military forces or promote the success of enemies of the United States. Palmer and Hoover orchestrated a series of well-publicized raids against any socialist supporter deemed capable of carrying out terrorist acts.

The "Palmer Raids" were conducted in over thirty cities nationwide with the arrests made by members of the Justice Department along with local police. The raids came without warning and focused on aliens rather than citizens whenever possible. Thousands of suspected radicals were arrested, most without proper arrest warrants and held without trial for up to four months. After investigation of each case by the Labor Department, the majority of those held were released.

In December 1919 only 248 of those arrested were actually deported. They were placed on a ship called the *Buford* bound for the Soviet Union. The public lost interest by the spring of 1920 as further terrorist attacks failed to materialize. By the fall when a bomb exploded on Wall Street, most American's considered the attack to be an assault by a deranged individual rather than a socialist conspiracy.

Earlier, while working at the Library of Congress, Hoover had mastered the Dewey decimal system (a numbering system for cataloguing library books) with its classifications and numbered subdivisions. Hoover decided to use that system as a model to create a massive card index of people with radical political views. Over time 450,000 names were indexed. Detailed biographical notes were written on the 60,000 he considered the most dangerous.

From these lists Hoover directed the arrests of suspected radical communists who were caught in the dragnet of the so-called "Palmer Raids" (raids in over thirty cities on aliens known or suspected of being political radicals resulting in thousands of arrests; see sidebar). From the court records in subsequent trials, Hoover also added to his files the names of hundreds of lawyers who had been willing to represent radi-

Hoover stands next to a map of the United States that shows his FBI agents throughout the country designated by numbered markers.
(© Bettmann/Corbis)

cals. His firsthand investigation of American and foreign communists, along with the intelligence files he began gathering, made him the government's first expert on domestic communism.

The Palmer Raids had the desired effect of reducing membership of the American Communist Party. Hoover was rewarded by being promoted to the post of assistant director of the Bureau of Investigation (BOI) in 1921. At that time the BOI employed mostly law school graduates and accountants and had limited power in law enforcement. The agency's main function was to investigate criminal violations of federal law.

Hometown advantage

Scandal and corruption—being bought off by criminals, particularly bootleggers, to look the other way—triggered reorganization of the bureau in 1924 and Hoover, at the age of twenty-nine, was named director. He set about establishing a world-class crime fighting organization. The first order of business was to reestablish and strengthen the chain of command. At the top of the agency was the Seat of Government (SOG), which was the Washington headquarters of the BOI, headed by the director and the assistant director.

He established a standardized system for all field offices and introduced personal standards for agents in dress as well as conduct. His special agents, known as "G-Men" (from government men), were ordered to wear the official uniform. This included a white shirt, dark suit, snap-brim hat, and a handkerchief in the jacket pocket.

Hoover obtained increased funding from Congress and proceeded to modernize the bureau. He built a world-renowned fingerprint identification unit, a pioneering crime laboratory, and a system for gathering and analyzing national crime statistics. In 1934, due to public reaction to gangster activity, Congress passed a package of nine major crime bills. These bills gave the federal government a comprehensive criminal code and Hoover's BOI a greatly expanded mandate, including counterespionage duties. The newly empowered bureau was renamed the Federal Bureau of Investigation (FBI) in 1935.

Personal changes were occurring at home for Hoover as well. His father died in 1935 and Hoover continued living with his mother until her death in 1938.

President Harry Truman (1884–1972; served 1945–53) pulled the FBI back into domestic intelligence investigations in 1947 when he created the Central Intelligence Agency (CIA) to deal with foreign intelligence. Angered, Hoover withheld cooperation, beginning a long history of animosity between the two agencies.

Hoover accumulated enormous power over the years, in part from his secret files that catalogued vast amounts of personal data on influential social and political leaders. The files, titled "Official/Confidential" (OC), were rumored but not

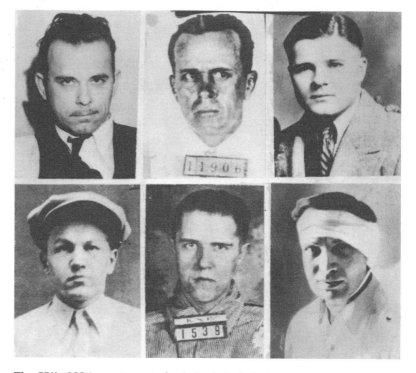

The FBI's 1934 most wanted criminals included many members of organized crime. FBI Director Hoover became a national hero during the 1930s with the FBI crackdown on notorious gangsters.
(© Bettmann/Corbis)

verified until after his death when his assistants destroyed them. He was a master of publicity and used everything from "junior G-man" clubs for boys, to his "ten most wanted" list, to the television series *The FBI,* to promote the Bureau. His power was sustained over the years by his uncanny understanding of the values, hopes, and fears of the vast majority of ordinary Americans.

As time passed Hoover became extremely sensitive to criticism, susceptible to flattery, and was feared both in and out of the bureau. His agents knew never to publicly criticize or embarrass the FBI or its director. Within the FBI, Hoover expressed his views on reports from assistants in bright blue ink reserved solely for his use. He would write in the margins of memorandums on all four borders around a typewritten sheet. Once an assistant filled the page to the edges so Hoover barely had room for a comment. He responded, "Watch the borders."

Puzzled but obedient, his aides dispatched agents to patrol the Canadian and Mexican borders for a week.

Hoover became a national hero during the 1930s with the FBI crackdown on notorious gangsters. Then during the 1940s and 1950s he was well known for his anticommunist views with the House Un-American Activities Committee (HUAC), an organization that relied heavily on information provided by the FBI. But Hoover began losing political support in the 1960s with his disregard for the Civil Rights movement.

The Civil Rights movement was a wide-ranging protest in the 1950s and early 1960s by private citizens contesting discriminatory laws against black Americans and city ordinances limiting their use of public facilities. The movement's civil disobedience strategies, including sit-ins blocking the access of others, boycotts of services, and demonstrations in the streets, led to direct confrontations with law authorities. Hoover's reputation was further damaged following revelations of his personal campaign to destroy civil rights leader Dr. Martin Luther King Jr.'s (1929–1968) career.

J. Edgar Hoover was director of the FBI from May 10, 1924, until his sudden death on May 2, 1972, at the age of seventy-seven. Both houses of Congress voted permission for Hoover's body to lie in the Capitol Rotunda for viewing by the public. Amid the eulogies, the Senate voted to name the new FBI building for the late director. J. Edgar Hoover was buried alongside his parents in Congressional Cemetery, just thirteen blocks from the row house where he had been born.

A Senate report in 1976 was highly critical of Hoover, accusing him of using the Justice Department to illegally harass political nonconformists in the United States. Many believed Hoover's long career included government abuse of authority and a disregard for individual civil liberties. Congress enacted legislation requiring Senate confirmation of future FBI directors and limited their terms to ten years.

For More Information

Books

Gentry, Curt. *J. Edgar Hoover: The Man and the Secrets*. New York: W. W. Norton & Company, 1991.

Hoover, J. Edgar. *Masters of Deceit: The Story of Communism in America and How to Fight It.* New York: Henry Holt and Company, 1958.

Sullivan, William C. *The Bureau: My Thirty Years in Hoover's FBI.* New York: W. W. Norton & Company, 1979.

Web Sites

"Crackdown!" *Smithsonian Magazine.* http://www.smithsonianmag.si. edu/smithsonian/issues02/feb02/red_scare.html (accessed on August 15, 2004).

"J. Edgar Hoover." *New York Times Obituary.* http://nytimes.com/learning/ general/onthisday/bday/0101.html (accessed on August 15, 2004).

Ted Kaczynski

Born May 22, 1942 (Evergreen Park, Illinois)

Domestic terrorist

Ted Kaczynski was an American terrorist who used his crimes to draw attention to his political views. His campaign to fight what he believed was the evil of technological progress was waged with bombs he delivered or mailed to sixteen different places across the country. Over a period of eighteen years, Kaczynski killed three people and wounded twenty-three others with his bomb devices. His primary targets were people he associated with computers and other high-tech industries.

Kaczynski believed that modern industrial civilization was destroying nature, alienating humans from one another, and manipulating people's minds and attitudes. In his writings, which became commonly known as the "Unabomber Manifesto," Kaczynski argued for the destruction of the industrial system in order to rid the world of modern technology and free humanity.

The education of a genius

Theodore John Kaczynski was born on May 22, 1942, in the Chicago, Illinois, suburb of Evergreen Park. Wanda Theresa Dombek and Theodore Richard Kaczynski soon discovered

"The Industrial Revolution and its consequences have been a disaster for the human race."

Ted Kaczynski. *(AP/Wide World Photos)*

that their little "Teddy" was gifted with an extremely high IQ. Ted was a shy boy who spent a great deal of his childhood indoors reading science magazines with his mother. By the time his brother David was born in 1950, Ted's father sought a recreational balance by teaching his boys how to live in the outdoors.

Young Ted breezed through school, skipping two grades and showing a talent for mathematics. He graduated from Evergreen Park High School at age sixteen and immediately entered Harvard University in Cambridge, Massachusetts, on a math scholarship. Because he was so much younger than

Domestic Terrorism

Americans were not unfamiliar with domestic terrorism when Ted Kaczynski began his attacks on modern technology in 1978. In April 1919 a series of bombings occurred associated with the notorious Red Scare, or communist threat that had shaken the nation's security. A total of thirty-eight package bombs were mailed to a variety of government officials and business leaders that spring.

A terrorist conspiracy was widely feared when the package bombs were followed by dynamite attacks in June of 1919. Explosions occurred at the homes of prominent leaders in a coordinated attack targeting eight major U.S. cities.

Ted Kaczynski used the U.S. Postal Service to send his package bombs from 1978 to 1995. His reign of terror was followed by a new form of killing beginning in October 2001 when anthrax-laced letters were mailed to several prominent addresses. Attacks such as these usually receive wide media coverage for a perpetrator's cause and are also an effective way to spread fear and anxiety among a large population.

In many cases, terrorists call officials or the media to claim responsibility for an act and to make their demands known on how to prevent further attacks. If no one claims responsibility for an attack, it remains a mystery for authorities to solve. That mystery creates a different kind of fear and suspicion. A lone terrorist is the most difficult to identify, predict, and prevent because he or she makes no contact with other terrorists.

the other students, Ted was viewed as an oddity and spent most of his time alone studying. He graduated in 1962 at the age of twenty and set off for graduate school. Ted earned a master's and a doctorate degree in mathematics from the University of Michigan over the next five years. His prizewinning dissertation (thesis) was on a pure mathematical problem about circles and equations.

In 1967 Kaczynski was hired as an assistant professor in the math department at the University of California at Berkeley. After only two years he suddenly quit his teaching post despite the university's desire to keep him on the faculty. Kaczynski returned to his parents' home near Chicago and applied for a Canadian land grant. While waiting for a response he worked various jobs and began writing antitechnology essays. When Ted was denied his request for immigration to Canada he headed into the wilderness of Montana.

In 1971 Ted and his brother David purchased a small parcel of land in Florence Gulch, just eighty miles southwest of Great Falls, Montana. The untouched area had more bears than people and was a perfect place for the intensely private Kaczynski. In 1975 he built the ten-by-twelve-foot cabin that would be his home for the next twenty years.

Ted's cabin lacked electricity and plumbing but required very little money for upkeep. He kept a small garden, hunted rabbits for food, and lived the life of a hermit. Kaczynski spent most of his time in the wilderness reading, writing, and developing his thoughts. At one point in 1978 he made the effort to return to society in Chicago, but it was not a good fit. By 1979 Ted was back at his cabin in Montana. He kept in touch with his family on occasion and in 1990 heard that his father had committed suicide after being diagnosed with cancer.

Defining the "Unabom"

On May 25, 1978, Kaczynski delivered a package bomb to a parking lot at the University of Illinois at Chicago. It was addressed to engineering Professor E. J. Smith, Rensselaer Polytechnic Institute in Troy, New York. It appeared to be an undelivered parcel returned to its sender—Professor Buckley Crist of Northwestern University in nearby Evanston, Illinois. Without questioning how it had arrived at a different institution, the finder contacted Professor Crist. Crist claimed to have no knowledge of the parcel but had it sent to him anyway. When he saw the package the following day, he noticed it hadn't been addressed in his own handwriting. This made him suspicious enough to call the campus police to investigate. A security guard was injured when he opened the package and it exploded. A year later, Kaczynski left a second bomb at the institute, which injured a graduate student who opened the package.

Kaczynski was back in Montana by mid-1979 where he worked on his manifesto (a public declaration of principles and aims, especially of a political nature) and improved his bombs. On November 15, 1979, a bomb exploded in the cargo hold of an American Airlines flight, requiring an emergency landing at Dulles International Airport near Washington, D.C.

This ten-by-twelve-foot cabin in Montana was Ted Kaczynski's home for twenty years. When the FBI arrested him there in 1996, they found the material he used to make his bombs as well as other incriminating evidence. *(AP/Wide World Photos)*

Twelve people suffered from smoke inhalation. So far no one had been killed by Kaczynski's bombs.

The following year, on June 10, the president of United Airlines was injured by a bomb explosion at his home in the Chicago area. By the mid-1980s several more campuses and airlines had been targeted. The Federal Bureau of Investigation (FBI) was convinced one individual was responsible for all of the bombings. Since serial bombers are mostly male, the authorities assumed it was a male in this case. They formed a task force to determine the bomber's motives in order to identify him.

The codename for the case was UNABOM, an acronym for the bomber's preference of targets, UNiversities and Airlines

BOMbings. The media followed the case closely and eventually nicknamed Kaczynski the "Unabomber."

The attacks turned deadly on December 11, 1985, when a computer store owner in Sacramento, California, picked up a package outside his business and it exploded killing him. Then in February 1987 a witness spotted the Unabomber placing a bomb outside a Salt Lake City, Utah, computer store. A police sketch of the man wearing a hooded sweatshirt and dark aviator sunglasses was widely circulated. The bombings stopped for the next six years.

When the attacks began again in June 1993 several bombings left their victims injured but alive. This changed again in December 1994 when an advertising executive in New Jersey opened a package that exploded and killed him. The final murder occurred on April 24, 1995, again in Sacramento, when the president of the California Forestry Association opened a package bomb addressed to the previous president of the association.

The Freedom Club

For nearly eighteen years, the Unabomber had operated without detection. In an anonymous letter to the *New York Times* in June 1993, Kaczynski explained his terrorist cause and demanded the *Times,* or another major newspaper, publish the manifesto he had written. He identified himself as a member of the "Freedom Club" and signed the letter "FC." The letter stated that if the newspaper agreed to publish his writings, the attacks would stop. If they did not agree to his demands, the attacks would intensify.

The FBI continued to search for the identity of the bomb maker. Their only breakthrough came when the letters "FC" were found carved on pieces of metal that had survived the blasts. Aside from the letters, the only other means of identifying the attacker was his consistent use of wood in making the bombs. The wood was an unusual touch since most pipe bombs usually use threaded metal ends that can be bought in any large hardware store.

With so little to go on the authorities agreed to the Unabomber's demands to publish the entire text of his 35,000-word manifesto. On September 19, 1995, the *Washington Post* and the *New York Times* both ran the piece entitled, "Industrial Society and Its Future." It became known as the "Unabomber Manifesto" and would ultimately be the clue needed to solve the case.

David Kaczynski read the manifesto and recognized his brother's writing style. Ted Kaczynski was arrested in April 1996 at his cabin in Montana. He was indicted in Sacramento and New Jersey for five Unabomber attacks, including the three deaths. Kaczynski was diagnosed as paranoid schizophrenic (a severe mental disorder that can include delusions and hallucinations) but declared mentally competent to stand trial. He agreed to plead guilty on January 22, 1998, to avoid the death penalty. He received four life sentences plus thirty years in prison without the possibility of parole. Kaczynski is incarcerated in the supermax prison in Florence, Colorado, for his eighteen-year crime spree.

For More Information

Books

Chase, Alton. *Harvard and the Unabomber: The Educations of an American Terrorist.* New York: W. W. Norton & Company, 2003.

Fridell, Ron. *Terrorism: Political Violence at Home and Abroad.* Berkeley Heights, NJ: Enslow Publishers, Inc., 2001.

Gottesman, Ronald, ed. *Violence in America: An Encyclopedia.* New York: Charles Scribner's Sons, 1999.

Web Sites

"Famous Nonmathematicians." *Loyola College in Maryland.* http://www.loyola.edu/mathsci/resources/famousnonmathematicians.htm (accessed on August 15, 2004).

"Should We Have Second Thoughts About Kacz[y]nski." *American Psychological Association.* http://www.apa.org/monitor/mar98/sp.html (accessed on August 15, 2004).

Estes Kefauver

Born July 26, 1903 (Madisonville, Tennessee)
Died August 10, 1963 (Bethesda, Maryland)

U.S. senator

"In the United States today, [many] . . . believe that if this country is to be kept great, the little man must be given an adequate opportunity and a reasonable standard of living. I'm on the side of the [these] . . . people."

Estes Kefauver was a senator from Tennessee who gained national attention as chairman of the Special Committee on Organized Crime in Interstate Commerce. Conducted by the Eighty-first and Eighty-second Congresses in 1950 and 1951, the committee was more commonly known as the "Kefauver Committee." Using the relatively new medium of television, the hearings drew public attention to the revelation that a nationwide organized crime syndicate actually existed. They also made the phrase "taking the Fifth" a part of American conversation, as many witnesses invoked their constitutional Fifth Amendment right against self-incrimination.

The five-man committee headed by Kefauver exposed a powerful underworld made up of mobsters and corrupt politicians. The hearings began in May 1950 and lasted for fifteen months. Sessions in fourteen cities heard testimony from hundreds of witnesses about violence, corruption, and the criminal control of illegal markets. The hearings resulted in Treasury Department indictments of hundreds of lawbreakers.

The Kefauver Committee submitted four reports indicating that organized crime syndicates existed through the sup-

Estes Kefauver. *(© Bettmann/Corbis)*

port or tolerance of public officials. It was not until 1970, however, that Congress passed the Organized Crime Control Act to coordinate the investigation and prosecution of organized crime in America.

A love of the law

Carey Estes Kefauver was born on a farm in Monroe County, near Madisonville, Tennessee. His mother was Phredonia Bradford Estes and his father, a hardware merchant, was Robert Cooke Kefauver. Estes attended public schools in the area and graduated from high school in 1922. He then went on to earn a Bachelor of Arts degree from the University of Tennessee at Knoxville in 1924. Kefauver left Tennessee to join the staff of a Hot Springs, Arkansas, high school where he taught mathematics and coached football for a year.

Kefauver then moved to New Haven, Connecticut, to attend law school at Yale University. He was admitted to the bar (the legal profession) in 1926, received a law degree with honors from Yale in 1927, and then returned to Tennessee to establish a law practice. Kefauver settled down in Chattanooga where he met Nancy Pigott of Glasgow, Scotland, while she was visiting relatives. The young couple married in 1935; they would become the parents of four children, one of them adopted.

Political persuasions

One of Estes Kefauver's clients was a local newspaper called the *Chattanooga News*. While serving as the paper's attorney over the years he developed an interest in politics. He sought election to the Tennessee senate in 1938. Though the campaign was unsuccessful, he was elected to the U.S. House of Representatives in 1939.

Kefauver spent the next nine years in the House where he was a consistent supporter of organized labor and other movements considered liberal (radical) in the South at the time (the South was more traditional and less open to progress and change). He focused most of his legislative efforts on congressional reform and antimonopoly measures (measures restricting businesses from controlling market prices for their goods). Kefauver established himself as one who did things on his own and who dedicated a great deal of energy and study into each area requiring his attention.

In 1948 Kefauver ran for the U.S. Senate as a Democrat. His campaign began with little public awareness or interest, while his opponent was well known and experienced. Kefauver began a new style of personal campaign by going town-to-town, meeting voters, and shaking their hands. Kefauver's sharp wit and sense of humor while interacting with people turned the tide of public support his way and was a dramatic high point of the campaign regarding the candidate's celebrity

Senator Estes Kefauver, seated second from left, during a Senate crime committee meeting in 1951. *(AP/Wide World Photos)*

status. His campaign strategy was successful and Kefauver was elected as the Democratic senator from Tennessee. He began serving on January 3, 1949, and would remain in the position until his death in 1963.

An honest man

Kefauver made his mark as a senator when he was appointed chair of the Special Committee on Organized Crime in Interstate Commerce. He headed the five-man panel and conducted hearings into the existence of a nationwide organized crime syndicate in the United States (see sidebar). The

Organized Crime

Organized crime thrives by providing goods and services that laws prohibit but people desire. Not everyone agrees about the seriousness of the various activities defined as organized crime. Not all Americans see sports betting, extortion (threats of violence), loan-sharking (charging very high interest rates on loans), and racketeering (participating in a pattern of more than one criminal offenses) as equally criminal or socially harmful. Organized crime, however, does use violence, intimidation, and threats to establish power. Corruption of police and public officials is necessary in sustaining control in criminal specialties, particularly involving drug trafficking and gambling.

Early in the nation's history, crime was seen by some immigrants and citizens at the city and regional levels as a practical avenue of upward social mobility. The bootlegging (selling illegal alcohol) and racketeering (obtaining money through illegal enterprise and often intimidation) of the 1920s expanded into labor unions in the 1930s and then casinos and real estate in the 1940s. By the 1950s gangsters were known to terrorize voters and manipulate local elections to their advantage.

The Kefauver Committee greatly increased public awareness of organized crime families in 1950 when it first exposed the powerful American Mafia or Cosa Nostra, literally meaning "our thing." Comprised of several influential Italian mob families, it was not the only crime organization in America,

investigation began in May 1950 and saw hundreds of witnesses testify in fourteen cities over the next fifteen months. Underworld figures from minor players to major gangsters as well as public servants, from police officers to mayors, gave testimony on the activities of organized crime.

Other congressional committees had been televised before but the Kefauver Committee was the first to attract a large audience. Because few people owned television sets during the 1950–51 hearings, they would gather in restaurants, bars, and businesses to watch the drama unfold. Never before had national attention been so completely focused on a single matter.

Kefauver encouraged the public trial to arouse the national sentiment necessary to pass legislation against organized crime. He agreed to respect the wishes of those who did not want to be televised when they were testifying. Kefauver was

as others existed. It was, however, the most powerful at the time.

In 1970 Congress passed the Organized Crime Control Act, also known as RICO (Racketeer Influenced and Corrupt Organization Act). It provided a coordinated effort in the investigation and prosecution of organized criminal groups. The Italian American crime families of the Mafia were not successfully prosecuted for their crimes until the 1980s and 1990s.

Congress passed RICO specifically to combat the infiltration of organized crime into legitimate businesses. Tougher penalties and increased protection for witnesses accompanied the Money Laundering Control Act of 1986. By the 1980s the definition of organized crime grew to include white-collar or corporate offenders, expanding the battle from the streets to the boardroom.

Criminal conspiracies in the 1980s included accountants, lawyers, bank officials, and real estate developers in a major savings and loan (banking) scandal. The late twentieth and early twenty-first centuries saw otherwise legitimate and official organizations committing organized crimes with far-reaching consequences.

Advances in communications technologies also increased international organized crime. The potential for committing crimes across borders further increased with the integration of the world's economic systems after the Cold War. (The Cold War was an intense political and economic rivalry from 1945 to 1991 between the United States and the Soviet Union falling just short of military conflict.) Governments were left to sort out political responses to the complexities of law enforcement as organized crime increasingly operated without national boundaries.

commended for protecting the constitutional rights of all witnesses during the investigation, while still successfully probing into organized crime in America.

The Kefauver Committee investigation produced significant results and offered several recommendations to Congress. Along with the formation of a racketeering squad in the Justice Department harsher penalties were created for many unlawful acts and efforts increased to deport gangsters. Over seventy local crime commissions were established in cities across America as public awareness of organized crime increased.

The great campaigner

To hundreds of thousands of Americans, Kefauver was the man who had exposed the darkness of organized crime and could be counted on to devote himself to the task of leading the nation. Riding on a wave of popularity, Kefauver ran for president in 1952 but lost the Democratic Party nomination. In 1956 he was chosen as Adlai Stevenson's (1900–1965) running mate in an unsuccessful bid for the White House.

Kefauver finally abandoned his presidential ambitions and returned to his legislative duties. In 1954 he took a courageous stand in supporting freedom of speech when he cast the sole senate vote in opposition to a bill outlawing the U.S. Communist Party. Kefauver sponsored a number of important foreign and domestic legislative measures. He continued his fight against monopolies as chair of the Senate Subcommittee on Antitrust and Monopoly from 1957 to 1963. The hearings covered organization and pricing practices of the steel, automobile, drug, and bread industries. The ensuing drug hearings sought to protect the public from harmful and ineffective pharmaceuticals. The investigation led to the Kefauver-Harris Drug Control Act of 1962, designed to guard against excessive pricing of prescription drugs.

Kefauver was in another antimonopoly debate in the Senate on August 8 when he became ill. He was taken to the naval hospital at Bethesda, Maryland, where he died two days later of a heart condition. Estes Kefauver was buried in the family plot in Madisonville, Tennessee.

For More Information

Books

Fontenay, Charles L. *Estes Kefauver: A Biography*. Knoxville, TN: University of Tennessee Press, 1980.

Hall, Kermit L. *The Oxford Companion to American Law*. New York: Oxford University Press, 2002.

Kefauver, Estes. *In A Few Hands: Monopoly Power in America*. New York: Pantheon Books, 1965.

Web Sites

"Happy 100th Birthday, Estes Kefauver!" *The University of Tennessee.* http://www.lib.utk.edu/spcoll/kefauver.html (accessed on August 15, 2004).

"Kefauver, Carey Estes, 1903–1963." *Biographical Directory of the United States Congress.* http://bioguide.congress.gov/scripts/biodisplay.pl?index=K000044 (accessed on August 15, 2004).

Kip Kinkel

Born August 30, 1982 (Springfield, Oregon)

Murderer

Kip Kinkel confessed to killing his parents on May 20, 1998, and then opening fire the following day at Thurston High School in Springfield, Oregon, killing two and wounding twenty-five. The following year he was sentenced to 111 years in prison. His case focused national attention on the continuing tragedy of school violence that plagued America in the late 1990s.

Special education

Kipland (Kip) Philip Kinkel was the second child born to Faith Zuranski and Bill Kinkel. His sister, Kristen, was nearly six years old when Kip was born in 1982. Both Bill and Faith were educators and took their children camping, hiking, and skiing almost every weekend. The Kinkel family moved to Spain for a year in 1986 and Kip entered his first year of formal schooling. His teacher did not speak English and it proved a difficult year for Kip.

Upon returning to Oregon Kip was enrolled at Walterville Elementary School in Springfield. He repeated the first grade due to his slow emotional and physical development.

"If Mr. Kinkel is sitting in prison without possibility of release for the rest of his life, it might—just might—keep some other young person from taking a gun to school. That would be the only positive thing that could come from this tragedy."

Mark Walker, father of Thurston victim Ben Walker

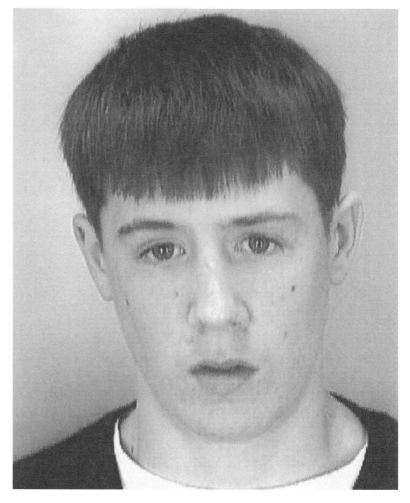

Police booking photo of Kip Kinkel. Kinkel was arrested after killing his parents, then going to his high school killing two people and wounding twenty-five others. *(AP/Wide World Photos)*

His parents enrolled him in karate classes where he did exceptionally well. Despite high IQ (intelligence quotient) scores, Kip continued to have problems in school and by third grade had qualified for special education services.

Kip's parents tutored him in the evenings when he fell behind at school. In addition, the family physician prescribed the drug Ritalin when it was decided he had attention deficit disorder, or ADD. (ADD is a learning and behavioral problem characterized by difficulty in sustaining attention and by impulse behavior. Ritalin is a drug that sometimes helps calm these symptoms.) There was also growing concern over Kip's interest in violence. The Kinkels disconnected their cable television service when they could no longer monitor Kip's viewing of violent programs.

In fourth grade Kip continued with special education and was diagnosed with dyslexia, a learning disability that interferes with the ability to recognize and comprehend written words. At the same time, however, he was placed in a Talented and Gifted program because he excelled in science and math. Despite being small for his age, Kip was good at sports in elementary school. Like his father, Kip was very competitive and had an uncontrollable temper.

In 1995 Kristen Kinkel transferred from the University of Oregon to Hawaii Pacific. No longer having his sister overseeing his activities, Kip began hanging out with a new group of boys and getting into serious trouble. Kip and three friends ordered bomb-building books over the Internet and began experimenting with explosives. One of Kip's friends sold him an old shotgun, which he kept hidden in his room. After several of the boys were caught shoplifting, the Kinkels pulled Kip out of Springfield's Thurston Middle School to tutor him at home for a year.

Criminal events continued in January 1997 when Kip joined a friend and his family on a trip to Bend, Oregon, for a snowboarding clinic. The two boys were arrested for throwing a twelve-inch rock onto a car from an overpass. Kip was taken into custody and his parents received a midnight call from the Bend Police Department. Once back home, the Kinkels put Kip in psychotherapy where he was diagnosed with major depressive disorder. Kip needed to learn more appropriate ways to manage his anger. His mother was concerned about Kip's extreme interest in guns, knives, and explosives.

Kip also had a strained relationship with his father, who was his disciplinarian since his mother thought Kip was a good kid who just had some bad habits. Both parents wanted him to take responsibility for the rock-throwing incident in Bend and, following a mandatory interview at the Skipworth Juvenile Facility, Kip was required to complete thirty-two hours of community service, write a letter of apology, and pay for damages to the car that was hit.

The Columbine Massacre

Eleven months after the Thurston tragedy, the scene was repeated in Littleton, Colorado. In April 1999 Columbine High School seniors Eric Harris and Dylan Klebold brought an arsenal of weapons into school and opened fire. The boys arrived at their school, located in an affluent Denver suburb, wearing trench coats and carrying automatic weapons. They wounded twenty-six students and killed thirteen others. Working their way through the school, they killed one teacher before finally turning the guns on themselves when it became apparent they would not escape. Both Harris and Klebold came from apparently normal and loving families.

The Columbine assault was widely publicized and refocused attention on the issue of school violence in America. The tragedy started a wave of so-called "copycat" violence in schools, where people mimic crimes committed by others. Early in the twentieth century, school discipline problems generally involved running in the hall and other unruly behavior. By the end of the century, school problems included weapons possession, gang activity, and violent assaults against students and teachers alike.

Sensational media coverage of suburban school killings was seen as increasing public awareness, but also encouraging the copycat phenomenon. The media filled the

Kip's final year in middle school ended in a two-day suspension for karate-kicking a schoolmate in the head for calling him names. Just three days later Kip received a three-day suspension for throwing a pencil at another boy. In June 1997 his psychologist recommended treatment with Prozac, an antidepressant drug. It seemed to be working well as both Kip's attitude and his grades began to improve. Kip remained on the drug the entire summer before he entered high school.

Thurston High School

Kip's fascination with firearms continued, however, and he begged his father to buy him a gun. Recently, Kip had secretly bought a .22-caliber pistol from a friend and kept it hidden from his parents. Bill Kinkel did not own any weapons but after resisting for some time decided on a new tactic. He reasoned that buying Kip a legally registered gun and teaching him how to properly use and care for it might decrease his son's fascination.

role of turning mass murderers into pop celebrities.

The Brady Handgun Violence Protection Act (Brady Law) was signed into law on November 30, 1993, in an effort to regulate increasingly powerful firearms. The Brady Law made it illegal for anyone under age twenty-one to purchase handguns from licensed dealers. The shooters at Columbine bypassed this problem by shopping at gun shows. Others, like Kip Kinkel, acquired guns by stealing them from their own homes or from the homes of others. The easy availability of weapons is of ongoing concern in the debate regarding school violence.

The identification of potentially violent and threatening students has become a priority in an attempt to reduce the incidents of school violence in the United States. A variety of areas have been singled out for study, including violence in popular music, television, and computer games. It was noted that kids playing point-and-shoot video games were getting the same training, and at a much younger age, as army recruits and police officers in America.

Exposure to violence is often made more severe by the availability of drugs, alcohol, and guns in schools. As the incidence of depression and suicide has increased among modern young people, so has the number of parents turning to mood altering drugs as an aid in parenting. The role of prescription drugs in the number of school shooters is a current topic for professionals in several fields searching for answers.

Father and son reached an agreement that Kip would do the research on the model he wanted and would pay for it with his own money. He was not to use the gun without his father and it would only become his when he turned twenty-one. The gun they purchased was a 9 mm Glock, just like the ones carried by many police officers.

Kip entered Thurston High School the fall of 1997. Things looked like they were going very well for the young freshman when the football coach invited him to tryout for the team. His sense of humor earned him attention as the class clown, and his social time was spent with a group of friends who called themselves "the good guys." Because he wanted to distance himself from more problems, Kip spent most of his time with this new group but maintained some contact with his old friends. Kip's parents believed things might be turning around for their troubled son.

The Kinkel home was in a rural area along the McKenzie River several miles from town. Kinkel's friends lived in town, closer to the school. He spent time with them there whenever possible. When alone at home, he spent hours walking up and down the road shooting birds and rodents with his shotgun and pistol. He boasted of his hunting exploits at school but no one paid much attention since most of the boys did the same.

When Kip gave a presentation in speech class titled "How to Make a Bomb," it seemed ordinary compared with many of the other topics presented. Likewise, Kip's continued talk of shooting things and blowing up the school seemed like more evidence of male bravado (trying to impress by acting tougher) and Kip's weird sense of humor.

A day of tragedy

Throughout the fall of 1997 and into 1998 the United States experienced a sudden outbreak of school shootings, each highlighted in the national media. Schools were on alert and there was little tolerance for weapons violations. On May 20, 1998, Kip and another freshman were arrested at Thurston High School on charges involving the possession and sale of a stolen handgun.

Kip was taken to the Springfield Police Station where he was fingerprinted and photographed. He was charged with five felonies, the most serious being possession of a firearm on school grounds. Among other things, Kip would be suspended from school for a year. Bill Kinkel picked his son up around noon and they stopped for lunch at a local restaurant. They agreed not to upset Kip's mother with the news while she was working. They would wait for her to get home that evening. Kip was especially sensitive to the fact that his parents were teachers and he had embarrassed them in front of their peers.

Father and son were home by 2:00 P.M. that afternoon and both received phone calls from friends. Bill Kinkel also made a call to the director of a residential program for troubled teens in Bend. Sometime between 3:00 and 4:30 P.M. that afternoon, Kip took a .22 rifle and shot his father in the back of the head from about ten feet away. He took the body into the bathroom and covered it with a white sheet, then waited for his mother to come home. Faith Kinkel arrived home from work around 6:30 P.M. Kip went down to the garage to help her

Kip Kinkel puts his head down in court while waiting to hear his sentence after he pleaded guilty to killing four people and injuring twenty-five others. *(AP/Wide World Photos)*

carry up groceries. He told his mother he loved her, then shot her several times and covered her body with a sheet.

Kip stayed up all that night and then drove his mother's car into Springfield. He arrived at Thurston High School around eight on the morning of May 21 and parked a block away. Wearing a long tan trench coat to hide the pistols in his waistband and the rifle at his side, Kip headed toward the school cafeteria. By the time he was wrestled to the ground by classmates, Kip had killed two students and wounded twenty-five more.

The trial

Less than twenty-four hours after his initial arrest, Kip Kinkel was back in the custody of the Springfield Police

Department. Secured in an interview room and locked in handcuffs, Kip managed to retrieve a hunting knife he had taped to his leg and attacked the returning detective. He was quickly subdued. During the ensuing interview, Kip confessed to killing his parents. The recovery of their bodies was delayed while officials disarmed a series of bombs in the Kinkel home, including one placed under his mother's body.

On May 22 Kip was arraigned and charged with four counts of aggravated murder, and in June he was indicted on an additional fifty-eight felony charges. Under a plea agreement entered September 24, 1999, Kip pled guilty to four counts of murder and twenty-six counts of attempted murder. The guilty plea eliminated a jury trial as well as the possibility of Kip being acquitted by an insanity defense.

Both sides had tried cases in Lane County before circuit court judge Jack Mattison and had found him to be fair. Before deciding Kinkel's sentence, the judge heard testimony from detectives and physicians as well as friends and family of both the accused and his victims. The defense presented a number of experts in an effort to prove Kip was mentally ill. After a six-day hearing, Kip Kinkel was sentenced to 111 years in prison without the possibility of parole.

Kinkel was immediately transferred to MacLaren Youth Correctional Facility, a state juvenile prison where violent offenders undergo a program of intensive therapy. Offenders remain at the facility until it is determined they are suitable for adult prison. Kinkel's defense team began a series of appeals. In January 2004, Kinkel's attorneys filed a petition seeking a new trial. The petition, filed in Marion County Circuit Court in Salem, Oregon, claimed evidence of Kinkel's mental illness had been disregarded at his trial.

For More Information

Books

Bonilla, Denise M., ed. *School Violence*. New York: H. W. Wilson Company, 2000.

Levinson, David, ed. *Encyclopedia of Crime and Punishment*. Thousand Oaks, CA: Sage Publications, 2002.

Periodicals

King, Patricia, and Andrew Murr, "A Son Who Spun Out of Control." *Newsweek* (June 1, 1998): pp. 32–33.

Sullivan, Randall, "A Boy's Life: Part I." *Rolling Stone* (September 17, 1998): pp. 76–85, 106–107.

Sullivan, Randall, "A Boy's Life: Part II." *Rolling Stone* (October 1, 1998): pp. 46–54, 72.

Web Site

"The Killer at Thurston High." *PBS Online and WGBH/Frontline.* http://www.pbs.org/wgbh/pages/frontline/shows/kinkel/kip (accessed on August 15, 2004).

Henry C. Lee

Born November 22, 1938 (People's Republic of China)

Forensic scientist

"The criminal investigator and forensic scientist are later responsible for scientifically finding the evidence which will clearly exhibit to a judge and jury just how a murder has been committed and by whom."

Dr. Henry C. Lee is an internationally respected authority in the field of forensic science. Forensic science refers to scientific testing methods and the latest technologies to the collect, preserve, process, and analyze evidence. He has worked with law enforcement agencies on thousands of crime scenes in over thirty countries around the world.

Throughout his career Lee has been called on to testify as an expert witness in numerous challenging and high-profile cases. Dr. Lee helped develop research methods to extract and analyze DNA (deoxyribonucleic acid) from human bones. DNA is microscopic genetic material found in a person's cells, which is unique to each person. This technological advance was used to identify bodies of U.S. soldiers recovered in Vietnam following the Vietnam War (1954–75; a controversial war in which the United States aided South Vietnam in its fight against a takeover by Communist North Vietnam). The technique also helped identify the remains of war victims recovered from a mass grave in Bosnia in the 1990s. In 1998 Lee founded the Henry C. Lee Institute of Forensic Science in order to advance the study and development of forensic science.

Dr. Henry C. Lee. *(AP/Wide World Photos)*

The need for knowledge

Henry C. Lee was born in the People's Republic of China on November 22, 1938. He grew up in Taiwan and attended the elite Taiwan Central Police College where he majored in Police Science. After graduating in 1960 Lee joined the Taipei Police Department. He became one of the country's youngest officers to attain the rank of captain. Henry and his wife, Margaret, immigrated to the United States in 1965 where he attended the John Jay College of Criminal Justice in New York City.

While pursuing his education, Lee worked at the New York University Medical Center from 1966 until 1975. In 1972 Lee graduated with a degree in forensic science then went on to New York University. His studies in biochemistry earned him a master's degree in 1974 and a Ph.D. in 1975. The Lees had a daughter named Sherry and a son named Stanley.

Upon completion of his doctorate, Dr. Lee joined the University of New Haven as an assistant professor. He created the school's forensic science department and also volunteered his services to the Connecticut State Police to develop a modern forensic science laboratory. In addition, Lee introduced the Major Crime Squad concept for criminal investigation to the state. By 1978, Dr. Lee earned the rank of full professor at the University of New Haven. The following year he was appointed as the first chief criminalist for the State of Connecticut, a position he held until 2000.

The future of science

Although ancient versions of forensic medicine date as far back as fifteenth-century China, the scientific investigation of crimes is largely a modern development. Not until the 1990s did significant advances in the field of forensic science take place. There are a variety of specialties under the broad umbrella of forensic science. One is criminalistics, which involves the collection and identification of such things as fingerprints, hair, fibers, blood, and DNA. Another is forensic medicine, which investigates the cause and manner of a death. Others include forensic toxicology (detecting of poisons); forensic dentistry (identification of bite marks); and forensic voiceprinting (identification through voice analysis). There are many other specialties as the science of forensics continually evolves.

Some forensic scientists search for and examine traces of material that might either prove or exclude an association between a suspect and a victim or a crime, called trace evidence. These traces might include blood, saliva and other body fluids, paint, glass, footwear and tire impressions, flammable substances and explosives, hairs and fibers. Others analyze drugs, specimens of tissue for poisons, and blood or urine for alcohol. Forensic scientists also examine firearms and documents and investigate the causes of fires, explosions, and road accidents.

Police agencies around the world have benefited from advances in forensic science and increasingly use them in their

Criminal Profiling

In the late 1960s the Federal Bureau of Investigation (FBI) established the Behavioral Science Unit (BSU), the first official department for criminal profiling in the United States. Criminal profiling is the development of an offender description by examining evidence. In 1972 a new FBI academy was opened in Quantico, Virginia, and the BSU became permanently based there. FBI profilers interviewed a number of existing prisoners in order to improve their techniques and better understand the minds of serial offenders. FBI profiler and investigator Robert Ressler published the results of this study in his book *Sexual Homicide: Patterns and Motives.*

Ressler's book is the main resource investigators use when they encounter a series of murders or sex crimes that appear to be linked. As an agent, Ressler also coauthored the FBI *Crime Classification Manual.* He coined the term "serial killer" and reported on his own interviews with many elusive murderers in his book entitled *Whoever Fights Monsters.* Ressler, John Douglas, and others helped develop the art of criminal profiling in the hopes of preventing future crimes and apprehending those who have already committed them.

Criminal profiling has a number of names such as "psychological profiling," "criminal personality profiling," and "behavioral crime scene analysis." The FBI refers to it as "criminal investigative analysis," and its profilers as "mindhunters." Profiling is a technique used to help law enforcement narrow its search when multiple suspects and multiple crimes exist. The offenders are not specifically identified but the major personality and behavioral characteristics of potential suspects are revealed.

Profilers examine crime scenes for clues that could suggest the type of person responsible. Details such as motivation, lifestyle, victim selection, and mental state can be gathered by a good profiler. In addition to physical evidence, profilers use police reports, crime scene photographs, and autopsy reports. Profilers make educated guesses in an investigation, but police agencies decide which evidence to use in solving actual crimes.

In 1984 President Ronald Reagan (1911–2004; served 1981–89) announced the formation of the FBI's National Center for the Analysis of Violent Crime (NCAVC). Its mission is to identify and track serial killers. At the same time the FBI's Violent Criminal Apprehension Program (VICAP) began. It was formed to link serial crimes across jurisdictions using a computer program. Profilers in the twenty-first century are increasingly called upon to investigate international crimes that can include dozens of physical locations and hundreds of individuals.

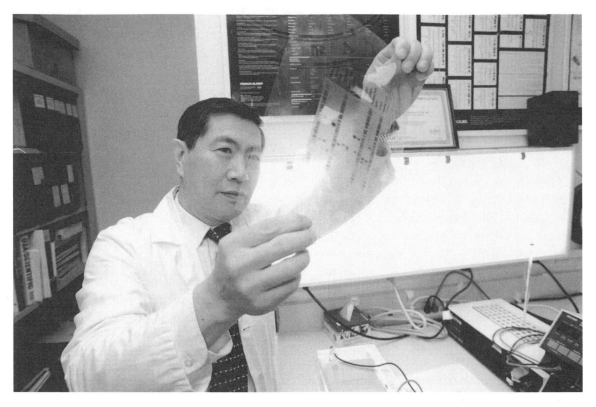

Dr. Lee examining a DNA profile. *(AP/Wide World Photos)*

investigations. The crime scene is where each investigation begins. The officers, detectives, and technicians must decide what types of evidence to collect. The crime scene can be as small as a room or as large as the three-mile path of a disintegrating airplane as it crashes to earth. It involves not only the actual location of the crime, but also the criminal's staging and planning areas.

Generally, the location of the original crime is considered a primary scene and any other locations are secondary. The crime scene includes both the area where the crime was committed, which must be secured and processed, as well as the people involved in the crime. This includes everyone from victims and survivors to witnesses and suspects.

Although the first response team decides what to collect and what to submit for laboratory analysis, the final decision on what type of physical evidence is submitted in court remains within the legal system. Prosecutors and defense attorneys decide what types of forensic evidence to use in criminal investigations and also which expert witnesses to call. Dr. Lee's testimony has been central to many major investigations —including the trial of football player O.J. Simpson in the murder of his wife and her lover; the murder of pageant star and child model JonBenet Ramsey; and the mysterious death of Vincent Foster, a high-ranking government lawyer and close friend of President Bill Clinton (1946–; served 1993–2001).

Dr. Lee has also been involved in the investigation, or in some cases the reinvestigation, of other famous cases, like the assassination of President John F. Kennedy (1917–1963; served 1961–63). In each case, Lee uses his forensic techniques to solve crimes and help bring criminals to justice.

Continuing the search

Dr. Lee has received many awards in his lifetime. In 1992 he received a special honor when he was elected a Distinguished Fellow of the American Academy of Forensic Science. In 1996 Lee received the Medal of Justice from the Justice Foundation, and in 1998 the Science and Engineer Association awarded him their Lifetime Achievement Award.

In 1998 Lee founded the Henry C. Lee Institute of Forensic Science to promote the advancement of forensic science. He served as Connecticut's commissioner of public safety from 1998 to 2000 and was chief for the Scientific Services in the state.

Lee remained a full professor at the University of New Haven into the twenty-first century and has served as a visiting professor at eight other universities. A widely published author, Lee remains active on the lecture circuit as well. In his 2002 book *Cracking Cases,* Lee thanked his 105-year-old mother, An-Fu-Lee, for her support and encouragement over the years for both himself and his twelve siblings.

For More Information

Books

Genge, Ngaire E. *The Forensic Casebook: The Science of Crime Scene Investigation.* New York: Ballantine Books, 2002.

Lee, Henry C., and Jerry Labriola. *Famous Crimes Revisited*. Southington, CT: Strong Books, 2001.

Lee, Henry C., and Thomas W. O'Neil. *Cracking Cases: The Science of Solving Crimes*. Amherst, NY: Prometheus Books, 2002.

Lee, Henry C., and Frank Tirnady. *Blood Evidence: How DNA Is Revolutionizing the Way We Solve Crimes*. Cambridge, MA: Perseus Publishing, 2003.

Ressler, Robert K., and Tom Shachtman. *I Have Lived in the Monster*. New York: St. Martin's Press, 1997.

Web Sites

Dr. Henry Lee: Forensic Science. http://www.drhenrylee.com/home.shtml (accessed on August 15, 2004).

"Dr. Henry Lee." *Lawrence County, Tennessee.* http://www.co.lawrence.tn.us/events/LawSeminar/2002/HenryLee_bio.htm (accessed on August 15, 2004).

"Interview: Dr Henry C. Lee." *Crime Library.* http://www.crimelibrary.com/criminal_mind/forensics/lee/1.html?sect=21 (accessed on August 15, 2004).

Belva Ann Lockwood

Born October 24, 1830 (Royalton, New York)
Died May 19, 1917 (Washington, D.C.)

Attorney

Belva Ann Bennett McNall Lockwood gained notoriety as the first woman to run for president in the United States. She was nominated in both the 1884 and the 1888 presidential races by the National Equal Rights Party. Lockwood is best remembered, however, as the first woman admitted to practice law before the Supreme Court of the United States. She was also the first woman to practice law in the lower federal court system.

As a lawyer in Washington, D.C., Lockwood exerted a great deal of political influence in both Congress and the courts. While she was most visible in her campaign to earn women's rights, especially the right to vote, Lockwood also lobbied Congress on a wide range of issues addressing injustice against a variety of groups. Lockwood was an avid pacifist (person opposed to the use of force) who served as a member of the nominating committee for the Nobel Peace Prize.

"Why not nominate women for important places? . . . We shall never have rights until we take them, nor respect until we command it."

Changing worlds

Belva Ann Bennett was the second of five children born to Hannah Green and Lewis Johnson Bennett. She was born

Belva Ann Lockwood. *(The Library of Congress)*

in October 1830 on a farm in Niagara County, New York. Belva did her chores on the farm and attended a one-room country school until she was fifteen. Poor family finances required her to get a job teaching at the country school to earn tuition to attend the Girls' Academy in Royalton. Belva graduated in May 1848 and married Uriah H. McNall that fall. The couple had a daughter in July 1849 and named her Lura.

In May 1853 Uriah died of complications from a sawmill injury. Left to raise their young daughter alone, Belva made the difficult decision to leave Lura in the care of her parents and move to Lima, New York, to pursue an education. She attended Genessee Wesleyan Seminary and then went on to Genessee College (later known as Syracuse University). Belva received a bachelor of science degree in 1857 and accepted a position as principal of Lockport Union School in New York. During her term, Belva introduced progressive ideas to the school's curriculum, including public speaking and physical activities for the girls. She soon learned that male teachers earned twice as much as women for the same work. Belva joined the campaign to obtain equal pay for women teachers. She also took advantage of an opportunity to attend a course in law offered by a local attorney.

Moving mountains

In 1866 Belva took Lura, now seventeen years of age, and moved to Washington, D.C. Belva taught school and campaigned as an active member of the National Woman Suffrage Association, an organization seeking voting rights for women. In 1867 she helped found the Universal Franchise Association, Washington's first suffrage group. After a year Belva opened a private, coeducational school called McNall's Academy where both she and Lura taught. It was one of the first private schools in the capital to accept both girls and boys. Belva married Dr. Ezekiel Lockwood in 1868 and the following year they had a daughter, Jessie. Little Jessie died eighteen months later of typhoid fever, an infectious, often fatal bacterial disease transmitted in contaminated food or water.

Ezekiel assumed responsibility for the academy and encouraged Belva to pursue her goal of earning a law degree. Belva applied for admission to the law school of Columbian College (later George Washington University) in Washington. She was rejected, however, because of her gender. While waiting for admission to another law school Belva continued to work for women's rights. In 1872 she drafted a successful bill giving female civil servants (government workers) equal pay for equal work.

After further rejections from Georgetown and Howard universities, Belva was finally admitted to the newly formed National University Law School of Washington in 1871. She completed her degree requirements in May 1873 but was denied her diploma because of her gender. After sixteen months Belva grew frustrated. She wrote to U.S. president Ulysses

Grant (1822–1885; served 1869–77), also president of the National University Law School, demanding her diploma. Her diploma arrived within days, signed by the faculty and President Grant himself. On September 24 Belva Lockwood was admitted to the District of Columbia bar and then to the District's supreme court.

A long way to go

Lockwood became very well known in Washington as she developed a successful law practice. She liked the practicality of getting around the city on the tall, three-wheeled tricycles that were becoming popular for men. The trikes were considered unladylike due to women's fashions at the time consisting of long skirts. Belva bought one anyway and had a special dashboard made to keep her skirts down.

Lockwood had plenty of legal cases but was not allowed to practice before any federal courts located in Washington. In April 1874 she had an important case to argue before the U.S. Court of Claims but was required to turn it over to a male attorney and the case was lost. Lockwood's appeal of the court of claims' ruling to the U.S. Supreme Court in 1876 was rejected. Lockwood believed if women had the right to practice law, then they should be entitled to follow the case to the highest courts in the country. She lobbied Congress in a campaign to pass a bill to allow women to speak in courts. The work of Lockwood and her supporters paid off in 1877 when her bill secured a place on the congressional calendar. It passed the Senate and was signed into law by U.S. president Rutherford Hayes (1822–1893; served 1877–81) on February 15, 1879.

On March 3, 1879, Belva Lockwood became the first woman admitted to practice before the Supreme Court of the United States. On March 6 Lockwood was also admitted to practice before the U.S. Court of Claims, making her the first woman to practice in federal courts.

A full life

Lockwood bought a twenty-room house in Washington and set up law offices on the first floor for herself and two other women attorneys. Lockwood took every type of case but specialized in back-pay claims and pension (retirement pay)

A group of women marching in favor of passing an amendment to give women the right to vote. Lockwood was a devoted supporter of attaining equal rights for women. *(The Library of Congress)*

cases. She was never without work. She was also a popular lecturer and her articles were frequently published in newspapers and journals. Lockwood continued her life work of arguing the cause of equal rights for women, especially the right to vote (see sidebar).

Although women could not vote in national elections in nineteenth-century America, no law prohibited women from running for public office. In 1884, and again in 1888, Lockwood was nominated for president of the United States by the National Equal Rights Party. She ran on a platform of equal opportunity, uniform marriage and divorce laws among the states, temperance (opposition to alcoholic beverages), and peace. Her campaigns were unsuccessful but her nominations led to an increase in speaking engagements, which allowed her to promote her causes.

Amendment XIX

The Nineteenth Amendment to the Constitution states, "The right of citizens of the United States to vote shall not be denied or abridged by the United States or by any state on account of sex. Congress shall have power to enforce this article by appropriate legislation." The amendment guaranteeing all American women the right to vote was the result of decades of effort by many people. Women and men alike worked tirelessly from 1878, when the amendment was first introduced in Congress, until its passage in the summer of 1920.

Those who championed a woman's right to vote used a variety of strategies. Besides joining others in lecturing, writing, and petitioning Congress, Belva Lockwood also challenged male-only voting in courts of law. Others used more militant tactics such as marches, civil disobedience, and hunger strikes to draw attention to their cause. All were met with intense opposition and sometimes hostility. The political balance began to change when President Woodrow Wilson supported an amendment to the Constitution in 1918. The House of Representatives passed the amendment in May 1919 and two weeks later the Senate followed. The U.S. Constitution was radically changed forever when the U.S. Secretary of State confirmed the official endorsement on August 26, 1920, and women were permitted to vote.

Lockwood continued working for women and equal rights as well as temperance and world peace. An early member of the Universal Peace Union (UPU), Lockwood served on the editorial board of its paper, the *Peacemaker*. She was also a lobbyist for the organization. In 1889 Lockwood was the UPU delegate to the first International Peace Congress in Paris where she delivered her address in French. She served as delegate at future International Peace Congresses in London, Milan, Antwerp, Berne, Budapest, and The Hague. Lockwood received many honors in addition to serving as a member on the nominating committee for the Nobel Peace Prize.

Lockwood continued to live and work in her Washington home where she maintained a thriving practice. Her most notable case came in 1906 when she represented the Eastern Cherokee Indians in a claim against the U.S. government. A treaty signed in 1835 resulted in the relocation of the tribe after the government purchased their land. The money, however, had never been paid. At seventy-five years of age Lockwood appealed to the U.S. Supreme Court and won an amount several times more than the original price.

Lockwood continued practicing law until she was seventy-six, when ill health forced her to retire. In 1916 Lockwood's final public speech was in support of President Woodrow Wilson's (1856–1924; served 1913–21) reelection. Belva Ann Lockwood died form complications of old age on May 19, 1917. Her funeral services were held at the Wesleyan Methodist Episcopal Church in Washington, D.C., and she was buried in the Congressional Cemetery. Three years after Lockwood's death, Wilson signed the Equal Suffrage Amendment into law. On August 26, 1920, the Nineteenth Amendment to the Constitution was ratified and women across the nation were certified to vote.

For More Information

Books

Brown, Drollene P. *Belva Lockwood Wins Her Case*. Niles, IL: Albert Whitman & Company, 1987.

Hall, Kermit L. *The Oxford Companion to American Law*. New York: Oxford University Press, 2002.

James, Edward T., Janet Wilson James, and Paul S. Boyer, eds. *Notable American Women 1607–1950: A Biographical Dictionary*. Cambridge, MA: Belknap Press, 1971.

Maddex, Robert L. *The U.S. Constitution A to Z*. Washington, DC: CQ Press, 2002.

Magnusson, Magnus, and Rosemary Goring, eds. *Cambridge Biographical Dictionary*. New York: Cambridge University Press, 1990.

Web Sites

"Belva Ann Lockwood: For Peace, Justice, and President." *Stanford Law School*. http://www.stanford.edu/group/WLHP/papers/lockwood.htm (accessed on August 15, 2004).

"Belva Lockwood." *The Learning Curve*. http://www.spartacus.schoolnet.co.uk/USAWlockwoodBelva.htm (accessed on August 15, 2004).

Arabella Mansfield

Born May 23, 1846 (Burlington, Iowa)
Died August 1, 1911 (Aurora, Illinois)

Attorney, social activist

"The theory of this Government from the beginning has been perfect equality to all the people."

Arguments of the Woman-Suffrage Delegates to the U.S. Senate Committee on the Judiciary on January 24, 1880

Arabella Mansfield sought equal opportunities for women in all aspects of U.S. society. She was an activist in the nineteenth century women's rights movement that spanned a range of issues from voting rights for women to the right of practicing law. As a result she became the first female lawyer in the United States. She passed the Iowa bar exam in 1869 and opened the way for other women to practice law. Within the year the Iowa legislature amended its statute to allow women and minorities to practice law in the state.

Although Mansfield never practiced law herself, she maintained her interest in legal proceedings and joined the National League of Women Lawyers in 1893, leading the way for others into careers in the law profession. A lifelong educator, Mansfield also campaigned for equal educational opportunities for women. She was inducted into the Iowa Women's Hall of Fame in 1980.

A commanding presence

Belle Aurelia Babb was born on the family farm near Burlington, Iowa, in 1846 and was called Belle by her family

134

and friends. She was the second child born to Mary Moyer and Miles Babb. Her brother, Washington Irving Babb, was born two years earlier and would be her lifelong friend. When the children were young their father left Iowa to follow the gold rush to California. He became superintendent of the Bay State Mining Company and died when a mine caved in on him in 1852.

Mary Babb moved her children to Mount Pleasant, Iowa, in order to provide them with the best education possible. Belle attended local schools and graduated from the Howe's Academy where she showed an early interest in studying law.

In 1862 Belle enrolled at Iowa Wesleyan University in Mount Pleasant and began using the name Arabella. She began college at a time when academic institutions were opening their enrollment to women since many men were away fighting during the American Civil War (1861–65; war in the United States between the Union [North], who was opposed to slavery, and the Confederacy [South], who was in favor of slavery). Belle graduated in three years and was the valedictorian (top ranking student of his or her class) at graduation. Her brother was salutatorian (second highest ranking student) of the same class. Belle went on to teach at Simpson College in Indianola, Iowa, for a year before she returned to Mount Pleasant to marry her college sweetheart, John Melvin Mansfield.

John was a professor at Iowa Wesleyan. He encouraged Belle in her legal studies as well as her suffrage work. Suffrage was the women's movement that worked to earn American women the right to vote. Belle was active at the state level and became a part of the national effort led by Susan B. Anthony (see sidebar). In canvassing Mount Pleasant to promote women's rights, Belle she was joined by Alice Bird, who soon became her sister-in-law.

Barred from law practice

The opening of colleges to women in the nineteenth century was not without controversy. Much debate existed over the place of higher education in women's lives. Women were seen as physically and mentally inferior to men in traditional education, including the study of law.

Prior to 1900, the most common way for anyone to study law was as an apprentice or clerk to a practicing attorney. Af-

Susan B. Anthony

Susan Brownell Anthony (1820–1906) was not only a famous activist for women's suffrage (voting rights) but a famous criminal defendant in her pursuit of the cause. She was an educator in upstate New York when she became convinced of the need to work for women's rights full time. She resigned from her job and began volunteering in temperance societies, to help women and children who suffered abuses from alcoholic husbands.

Anthony also devoted her time to the antislavery movement from the early 1850s until the outbreak of the American Civil War in 1861. She served as an agent for the American Antislavery Society. In 1851 Susan met Elizabeth Cady Stanton (1815–1902), a national leader in social reform for women. She joined forces with Stanton and others to promote women's rights, which included the right to vote.

From 1868 to 1870 Anthony published the weekly magazine, *The Revolution*. The publication centered on the Women's Suffrage Association agenda and featured editorials written by Stanton. The magazine called for women's rights, including equal pay and the right to vote. Campaigns for women having a voice in the courtroom and at the ballot box were occurring simultaneously across the nation. When Arabella Mansfield became the first American woman admitted to the bar, *The Revolution* celebrated her achievement in print and praised her contribution to the women's movement.

In 1869 the women's rights movement split into two factions with Anthony and Stanton heading the more radical National Woman's Suffrage Association (NWSA) out of New York. They argued that full citizenship for women included the right to vote guaranteed to women in the U.S. Constitution. Their objective was to achieve voting rights for women through an amendment to the Constitution.

The NWSA did not use membership to promote its cause but attracted recruits through publications and annual conventions. Anthony herself made personal appeals for signatures on petitions and traveled the lecture circuit giving interviews to local newspapers.

ter sufficient study the prospective lawyer would take an oral exam administered by a local bar committee (a group of law officials responsible for testing new prospective lawyers to determine if they qualify to practice). If successful, he (the practice was not available to women) would receive a license to practice law in that state. Though standards in licensing var-

Susan B. Anthony. *(The Library of Congress)*

Some women had actually been successful in registering to vote but had been turned away by officials when they had tried to cast their ballots. On November 1, 1872, Susan B. Anthony and several others registered to vote in Rochester, New York. On November 5, Anthony showed up at the polls and the inspectors agreed to accept her vote. Two weeks later she was arrested at her home and charged with illegal voting.

Anthony was indicted on January 24, 1873, and entered a not guilty plea. While awaiting trial she engaged in a highly publicized lecture tour to draw attention to the issue. Her trial was held before Judge Ward Hunt on June 17 and 18 in Canandaigua, New York. Anthony was found guilty of violating the voting laws and fined one hundred dollars plus the cost of prosecution. Although tried and convicted, Anthony succeeded in her refusal to pay the fine.

Susan B. Anthony spent the rest of her life as a political reformer, working to guarantee women in the United States the right to vote. She wrote the Federal Woman Suffrage Amendment that was introduced in Congress in 1878. She took the fight to a larger audience when she organized the International Council of Women in 1888 and the International Woman Suffrage Alliance in 1904.

Anthony did not live to see the consummation of her efforts. She died at her home in Rochester, New York, on March 13, 1906. The Nineteenth Amendment to the Constitution guaranteeing American women the right to vote was not adopted until August 26, 1920.

ied greatly from state to state, states consistently excluded women from joining the bar.

A first for women

After her marriage, Mansfield joined her husband as a faculty member at Iowa Wesleyan where she taught English and

A session of the National Woman's Suffrage Association during a Chicago political convention in 1880. Arabella Mansfield was a suffragist and an activist in the nineteenth-century women' rights movement. *(© Bettmann/Corbis)*

history. She and John began studying law together in hopes of passing the bar exam. Mansfield spent additional hours preparing for the exam as an apprentice at Ambler's law office where her brother Washington worked before his own admission. When she felt confident she had mastered the material, the twenty-three-year-old Mansfield applied to be admitted to the Iowa bar in June of 1869. She passed the exam with high scores but had to take her situation before a judge in order to be admitted to the Iowa bar.

Iowa law stated only white men over the age of twenty-one were allowed to receive a law license. Judge Francis Springer was an advocate of women's rights and was looking for a way to support professional women. He interpreted the word "men" in the state statute to mean all humans. He declared that including males did not mean excluding females.

In 1869 Arabella Mansfield became the first woman lawyer admitted to the practice of law in the state of Iowa, as well as the United States. By March 1870 Iowa became the first state to officially amend its attorney licensing code as three other women were admitted. Mansfield's accomplishment was highly praised and a major achievement of the women's rights movement.

Educator and administrator

Mansfield continued her academic career at Iowa Wesleyan. Belle earned a master's degree in 1870 and a bachelor of laws (LLB) degree in 1872 from the same institution. She was a charter member of the Iowa Woman Suffrage Society whose convention met in Mount Pleasant in 1870. Using her law degree as a badge of respect, Mansfield went on the lecture circuit for the Iowa Peace Society, speaking about government and women's rights. She billed herself as "Belle Mansfield, Esq." for the tour.

In 1879 the Mansfields moved to Greencastle, Indiana, to join the faculty at DePauw University. John suffered a mental breakdown around 1883 and Belle took a leave of absence to care for him. He was eventually institutionalized in Napa Valley, California, and died in 1894. Belle never spoke of his illness in public. She returned to DePauw in 1886 where she taught but also devoted her energy to administration of the school. Mansfield eventually became dean of women and dean of the schools of art and music at DePauw.

End of an era

Mansfield continued her campaign for educational reform and equal opportunities for women. As a skilled debater, she was tireless in her efforts to ensure women received the right to vote. She was active in the Methodist Church in Greencastle and held a lifelong commitment to volunteer work in her community. In the summer of 1909 Mansfield took a voyage to Japan. While there, she discovered she had cancer. She returned to DePauw to complete one more year at the university before she was forced to retire due to ill health.

Arabella "Belle" Mansfield died at her brother's home in Aurora, Illinois, on August 1, 1911. She was buried next to her mother at Forest Home Cemetery in Mount Pleasant, Iowa. Mansfield died nine years before women in the United States obtained the right to vote.

For More Information

Books

Drachman, Virginia G. *Sisters in Law*. Cambridge, MA: Harvard University Press, 1998.

Edwards, Thomas G. *Sowing Good Seeds: The Northwest Suffrage Campaigns of Susan B. Anthony*. Portland, OR: Oregon Historical Society Press, 1990.

Epstein, Cynthia Fuchs. *Women in Law*. Urbana, IL: University of Illinois Press, 1993.

Web Sites

"Arabella Mansfield." *The State of Iowa*. http://www.state.ia.us/government/dhr/sw/iafame-mansfield.html (accessed on August 15, 2004).

"Arabella (Belle) A. (Babb) Mansfield—Timeline." *Stanford University*. http://www.law.stanford.edu/library/wlhbp/papers/BelleMansfieldTimeline.pdf (accessed on August 15, 2004).

"Stanton and Anthony Papers Project Online." *Rutgers University*. http://ecssba.rutgers.edu (accessed on August 13, 2004).

"The Susan B. Anthony Trial: A Chronology." *University of Missouri*. http://www.law.umkc.edu/faculty/projects/ftrials/anthony/sbahome.html (accessed on August 15, 2004).

Daniel McNaughtan

Born c. 1812 (Glasgow, Scotland)
Died May 3, 1865 (Berkshire, England)

Murderer

D aniel McNaughtan was tried in 1843 for the murder of a British government official. He was found not guilty by reason of insanity, and his case created a widely used legal precedent known as the McNaughtan Rules. These rules, established by Great Britain's House of Lords, were delivered by Chief Justice Nicholas Tindal (1776–1846), the judge who had presided at McNaughtan's trial. The rules state that: (a) every person is assumed to be sane until proven otherwise; and, (b) it must be clearly proved that at the time of committing the crime, the accused lacked the understanding to know the nature of his act or even that he was doing something wrong. To this day most American state criminal justice systems use a form of the McNaughtan Rules to determine a person's criminal responsibility.

McNaughtan's name has seen various spellings over the years, partly because people at that time did not always spell their names the same way in every document. In association with both the man and the rules, McNaughtan has appeared many ways including McNaughton, M'Naghten, MacNaughten, and McNaughtun. Financial records of Daniel's father,

"The test for sanity . . . is not one of whether the accused suffers from any mental disorder or not, but rather of whether his mental state is such that he should fairly be held responsible."

A basic description for the test for a criminal defendant's sanity

along with an 1843 newspaper article bearing the accused signature indicate that the McNaughtan spelling was the one used most by the family.

Learning right from wrong

Daniel McNaughtan was born in Glasgow, Scotland, to a poor dressmaker named Ada. Births were not required to be recorded in the Scottish Register Office until 1855, so the actual date of Daniel's birth is unknown. It has been estimated that he was born as early as 1812 or as late as the spring of 1813. Daniel was raised by his mother until her death in 1821 when he went to live with his father. His father, also named Daniel, was a respected businessman who owned several properties in addition to the wood turning (fashioning wooden pieces or blocks into various shapes) shop where he worked on Stockwell Street in Glasgow.

Daniel's stepmother resented his presence, but the ten year old became an apprentice to his father as a wood turner and proved to be very talented at the trade. After more than four years, Daniel became a journeyman (one level up from apprentice) and spent the next few years perfecting his craft. Daniel had a gentle temperament and a good work ethic, which made him a favorite among the other shopkeepers on Stockwell Street. When Daniel turned eighteen he was ready to become a partner with his father. His stepmother preferred that her own sons be given the business, so he remained only an employee.

Daniel continued working but at night went to school to prepare himself for a career on the stage. He studied the works of English playwright William Shakespeare (1564–1616) and several English dramatists until he was a competent actor. In 1832, at the age of nineteen, Daniel had enough money saved from work to pursue his theatrical career. He took the stage name of Mr. Knight and joined several others in a series of readings and recitations in the Glasgow Trades Hall. Joining a band of touring actors, Daniel found himself at various towns in western Scotland. The touring ended unsuccessfully and he returned to Glasgow three years later. He had become an accomplished reader and an effective public speaker but finances forced him to return to the more profitable trade of wood turner.

In 1835 McNaughtan opened his own small shop on Stockwell Street, just a few yards from his father's shop. He continued his education in science and the arts and taught himself French, wrote poetry, and enjoyed quoting Shakespeare to his fellow craftsmen. McNaughtan's skills kept him working steadily and his shop was busy. Most of Glasgow, however, was experiencing an economic recession and the trades were particularly hard hit. By the early 1840s, Great Britain was in a depression and even McNaughtan could not keep his shop going full time.

A downward spiral

In the fall of 1842 McNaughtan booked passage to London on the steamship *Fire King.* He secured a room in a boardinghouse and for the next sixteen weeks acquainted himself with the public offices and residences around 10 Downing Street. For three weeks McNaughtan studied the daily habits of the man he thought to be the prime minister, Sir Robert Peel (1788–1850).

On Friday, January 20, 1843, McNaughtan followed Edward Drummond as he emerged from the public offices on Downing Street. Drummond was the private secretary to the prime minister and resembled Robert Peel in stature and age. The two men were often mistaken for one another by the public. They kept the same schedule and there was no pictorial press available for people to distinguish one from the other in the nine-

Insanity Defense

Under the U.S. Constitution, a person is presumed innocent until proven guilty when charged with a crime. It is the duty of the prosecution to prove the accused is guilty beyond a reasonable doubt in criminal trials. Criminal prosecution in America allows for "justifications" or "excuses" for the defendant's crime.

A "justification" defense allows for the possibility that some situations require a person to choose between the lesser of two evils in deciding on an action. Self-defense is an example of justification. The degree and type of punishment is considered when there is a justification defense. Legal excuses, such as insanity, cover the other major type of criminal defense. If the accused is determined to be irresponsible, a successful defense in a court of law will receive a verdict of not guilty by reason of insanity. The person will not be punished but will be committed to a secure mental health facility until it is determined he or she is no longer mentally ill or dangerous to society.

Most states use a form of the McNaughtan Rules to determine a person's legal responsibility for a crime. Some states have added additional elements and others have abolished the insanity defense entirely. John Hinckley (1955–) was acquitted of murder by reason of insanity when he made an assassination attempt on U.S. president Ronald Reagan (1911–2004; served 1981–89) in 1981. As a result, Congress enacted a stricter insanity test that is now used in all federal criminal prosecutions.

A 1735 engraving by William Hogarth entitled *Rake's Progress: Scene at Bedlam.* Daniel McNaughtan occupied an eight-foot by ten-foot stone cell in Bedlam for twenty-one years. (*© Burstein Collection/Corbis*)

teenth century. Drummond walked to his bank and was returning to Downing Street when McNaughtan drew a pistol from his pocket and shot him in the back. He was reaching for a second pistol when a policeman wrestled him to the ground. Drummond survived for four days before he died from his wounds.

McNaughtan was taken to the station house at Gardener's Lane where he was charged with attempted murder. Six weeks later, on March 3, 1843, the thirty-year-old McNaughtan stood trial for the willful murder of Edward Drummond. The courthouse was packed with curious observers, including author **Charles Dickens** (1812–1870; see entry). McNaughtan entered a plea of "not guilty," and the trial began.

The prosecution's case centered on the fact that McNaughtan had shot the wrong man, which showed evidence of his diminished mental capacity. The lead attorney then offered his observations on the law of insanity to the court. The defense acknowledged McNaughtan had shot Drummond and stated its case would rest upon his state of mind at the time McNaughtan committed the offense.

Seven medical examiners testified for the defense that McNaughtan showed signs of insanity. The judge stopped the trial based on the medical evidence and instructed the jury, who returned a verdict of not guilty on the ground of insanity in less than two minutes. On March 13 McNaughtan was escorted to London's Bethlem Hospital at Newgate Prison, known locally as Bedlam. McNaughtan occupied an eight-foot by ten-foot stone cell that would be his home for the next twenty-one years. In 1864 he was transferred to the new State Criminal Lunatic Asylum at Crowthorne in Berkshire. He died the next year after twenty-two years of confinement. He was buried on the asylum grounds in an unmarked grave.

The McNaughtan Rules

Following McNaughtan's trial a great debate rose over the need for a more precise statement for the use of the insanity defense. The verdict alarmed the public and the government called on the judges of the Supreme Court of Judicature to present opinions on the law. The House of Lords presented judges with a series of questions they were to consider as a test of insanity. The judges' answers became known as the McNaughtan Rules, which outline the criminal responsibility of the insane in English law. The rules have been followed in many British Commonwealth countries and parts of the United States, but not in Scotland.

For More Information

Books

Hall, Kermit, ed. *The Oxford Companion to American Law.* New York: Oxford University Press, 2002.

Katsh, Ethan M., and William Rose, eds. *Taking Sides: Clashing Views on Controversial Legal Issues.* Guilford, CT: Dushkin Publishing Group, 2000.

Levinson, David, ed. *Encyclopedia of Crime and Punishment.* Thousand Oaks, CA: Sage Publications, 2002.

Moran, Richard. *Knowing Right from Wrong: The Insanity Defense of Daniel McNaughtan.* New York: The Free Press, 1981.

Walker, David M., ed. *The Oxford Companion to Law.* New York: Oxford University Press, 1980.

Web Site

Pearse, O'Malley. "Psychiatry and the Legal System." *The Irish Medical Journal.* http://www.imj.ie/news_detail.php?nNewsId=1573&nCatId=24&nVolId=85 (accessed on August 15, 2004).

Ernest Miranda

Born March 9, 1940 (Mesa, Arizona)
Died January 31, 1976 (Phoenix, Arizona)

Robber, rapist, murderer

Ernesto Miranda was a career criminal whose name became familiar to every American following a Supreme Court decision that created what became known as the Miranda Rights. Miranda's conviction in an Arizona court in 1963 would be overturned by the U.S. Supreme Court in 1966. In *Miranda v. Arizona* the Court determined Miranda's Fifth Amendment rights against self-incrimination had been violated during a police interrogation. This Court decision was one of several important rulings identifying legal safeguards for defendants in the criminal justice system.

> "You have the right to remain silent. Anything you say can and will be used against you in a court of law."
>
> *The beginning of the Miranda Rights*

Life of crime

Ernesto Arturo Miranda was born in 1940 and grew up in Mesa, Arizona. He was called Ernie as a youth but went by Ernest as an adult. He was the fifth son of Manuel A. Miranda, a house painter who had immigrated to the United States from Sonora, Mexico, as a child. Ernie's mother died when he was five years old and his father remarried the following year. Ernie did not develop a close relationship with his stepmother and drifted apart from his father and older brothers.

Ernest Miranda. *(AP/Wide World Photos)*

Miranda was absent from the Queen of Peace Grammar School as often as he attended, and by eighth grade he had dropped out of school entirely. He was detained that year for felony car theft and put on probation. The following year Miranda was arrested for burglary and sent to Arizona State Industrial School for Boys at Fort Grant. He was released in December 1955 only to be sent back to Fort Grant in January 1956. This time he was arrested for attempted rape and assault.

When he was released a year later, Miranda moved to Los Angeles. By the fall of 1957 the teenager found himself imprisoned for the third time in less than three years when he was picked up on suspicion of armed robbery and placed in the custody of the California Youth Authority. Upon his release Miranda was sent to Arizona where he joined the U.S. Army in April 1958.

Miranda soon went AWOL (absent without approved leave) and was caught in a "peeping Tom" charge (watching someone without their knowledge). This earned him six months of hard labor in the military post stockade at Fort Campbell, Kentucky. He received an undesirable discharge in July of 1959 at the age of nineteen.

Criminal justice

Miranda's life of crime continued. He was arrested March 13, 1963, in Phoenix, Arizona, as a suspect in the armed robbery of a bank worker. While in police custody, Miranda signed a written confession to the robbery, as well as the kidnap and rape of an eighteen-year-old woman in the desert outside Phoenix. The police interrogated Miranda for two hours without advising him he had the right to remain silent or to have an attorney present during questioning. The police form he signed was a preprinted warning of rights with a blank for the name of the person making the statement. Signing the form indicated the confession he gave was voluntary, making it admissible in court.

On March 14 Miranda was taken before a city magistrate and charged with failure to register as an ex-convict. He was sentenced to ten days and transferred to the county jail. This allowed police time to hold him while investigating the more serious charges. They soon charged Miranda with robbery, kidnapping, and rape. He was assigned an attorney to defend him at trial.

Ernest Miranda was convicted of robbery on June 19, 1963, in Maricopa County Superior Court. The following day his trial began for the kidnapping and rape charges. Miranda's confession was admitted into evidence and the jury deliberated for five hours before returning a guilty verdict on June 27. Miranda received two concurrent terms in the Arizona State Prison at Florence. He received twenty to thirty years for each of the charges against him.

In December 1963 Miranda's attorney appealed to the Arizona Supreme Court on the grounds that Miranda did not

Earl Warren

Earl Warren graduated from the University of California in 1912 and received a law degree two years later. He first practiced law in San Francisco and Oakland. In 1919 Warren began a life in public service when he became deputy city attorney of Oakland. In 1920 he became deputy assistant district attorney of Alameda County. Warren served as district attorney of Alameda County from 1925 until 1938.

Warren was elected attorney general of California in 1938 before serving three terms as the state governor beginning in 1942. President Dwight D. Eisenhower (1890–1969; served 1953–61) nominated Earl Warren as chief justice of the U.S. Supreme Court in 1953, a position he held until his retirement in 1969. Warren chaired many notable cases during his tenure, including the commission investigating the 1963 assassination of President John F. Kennedy (1917–1963; served 1961–63).

Warren's Court decisions worked toward fairness in criminal proceedings. Earlier courts had emphasized property rights, but under Warren the Court focused more on individual rights, especially those guaranteed by the U.S. Constitution. During his early years as an attorney in criminal justice, Warren had recognized the possibilities for police abuse during pretrial interrogations. He argued that reform was needed to ensure American citizens were duly informed of their rights when accused of committing a crime.

know he was protected from self-incrimination and that he had been tricked into confessing to the crimes. By February 1966 the case had made its way to the U.S. Supreme Court under Chief Justice Earl Warren (1891–1974; see sidebar).

Miranda rights

After hearing arguments in the *Miranda v. Arizona* case, the Supreme Court overturned Miranda's conviction on June 13, 1966. The landmark ruling confirmed that in order for a confession to be admissible in a court of law it must be given voluntarily. It was determined that Miranda had not been informed of his rights before he signed the confession. Chief Justice Warren wrote the Court ruling that outlined how law enforcement must handle defendant interrogations during an investigation. Fair interrogation procedures of crime suspects,

Supreme Court Justice Earl Warren. *(The Library of Congress)*

The Fifth Amendment to the Constitution states, "No person . . . shall be compelled in any criminal case to be a witness against himself." The rules used to determine whether a confession of guilt was voluntary or forced were vague. Chief Justice Warren led the Supreme Court as they began to look for cases that would enable them to give a clearer, more meaningful rule to define a voluntary confession. Several cases where a defendant had not been adequately advised of his or her rights were reviewed by the Court in the mid-1960s. *Miranda v. Arizona* was one such case reviewed in 1966. The Court determined Miranda's Fifth Amendment right against self-incrimination had been violated. The Supreme Court handed down its opinion on June 13 and it contained what is now referred to as the "Miranda Rights."

while in police custody, had to begin with what became known as the Miranda Rights.

The Court did not specify the exact wording in its decision but did require that the warning must be given once an individual had been taken into custody before they are interrogated. Over time a simple version of the warning was printed on wallet-sized cards and distributed to police departments so the wording was consistent. It was later reported that Miranda kept copies of the cards in his wallet and would sign them for a fee.

The so-called Miranda Warning changed little over time. It became familiar to the public thanks to the numerous police and detective shows on television and in movies that used it in their scripts. The Miranda Warning included the following four rights: (1) you have the right to remain silent; (2) anything you say can and will be used against you in a court

WARNING

The constitution requires that I inform you of your rights:

You have a right to remain silent. If you talk to any police officer, anything you say can and will be used against you in court.

You have a right to consult with a lawyer before you are questioned, and may have him with you during questioning.

If you cannot afford a lawyer, one will be appointed for you, if you wish, before any questioning.

If you wish to answer questions, you have the right to stop answering at any time.

You may stop answering questions at any time if you wish to talk to a lawyer, and may have him with you during any further questioning.

Rev. 9-79

A copy of the Miranda Rights, a warning that all police officers must give people being arrested.

---

of law; (3) you have the right to speak to an attorney, and to have an attorney present during any questioning; and (4) if you can not afford an attorney, one will be provided for you at government expense.

The Supreme Court ruling was received with mixed reviews and became controversial. Some saw it as lending dignity to the suspect in the legal system and others saw it as weakening the ability of law enforcement to fight crime. Most saw it as an effort to strike a proper balance between the two.

Final justice

The Supreme Court decision did not free Miranda but offered him a new trial without the confession he made to the police. Ernesto Miranda's second trial for rape and kidnapping opened in mid-February 1967 at the Maricopa County Superior Court. This time his common-law wife testified that Miranda had confessed to the crime when she visited him in prison in 1963. (A common-law marriage is when a couple who can prove they have lived together for a certain period of time are considered legally married in some states under certain conditions.) He had asked her to make a personal appeal to the victim in order to have the charges dropped. The jury deliberated for an hour and twenty-three minutes before finding Miranda guilty. He was sentenced again to twenty to thirty years in the Arizona State Prison at Florence.

Released on early parole in December 1972, Miranda was back in prison by 1975 on yet another charge. In 1976 Miranda ended up in a Phoenix bar fight and was stabbed to death. The man suspected of killing him chose to exercise his right to remain silent after being read his Miranda Warning. He refused to talk to the police and, due to a lack of witnesses or other physical evidence, was never charged with Miranda's murder. Ernesto Miranda was buried at the Mesa City Cemetery in Arizona.

For More Information

Books

Baker, Liva. *Miranda: Crime, Law and Politics*. New York: Atheneum, 1983.

Cushman, Clare, ed. *The Supreme Court Justices: Illustrated Biographies, 1789–1993*. Washington, DC: CQ Press, 1993.

Hall, Kermit L., ed. *The Oxford Guide to United States Supreme Court Decisions*. New York: Oxford University Press, 1999.

Leo, Richard A., and George C. Thomas III, eds. *The Miranda Debate: Law, Justice and Policing*. Boston, MA: Northeastern University Press, 1998.

Mauro, Tony. *Illustrated Great Decisions of the Supreme Court*. Washington, DC: CQ Press, 2000.

Web Site

"Ernesto Miranda." *Doney & Associates Lawyers*. http://www.doney.net/aroundaz/celebrity/miranda_ernesto.htm (accessed on August 15, 2004).

Allan Pinkerton

Born August 25, 1819 (Glasgow, Scotland)
Died July 1, 1884 (Chicago, Illinois)

Private investigator

"The role of detective is a high and honorable calling."

From the Pinkerton National Detective Agency's code of conduct

Allan Pinkerton provided America with a national policing system at a time when there was little federal or state law enforcement. Credited as a reformer for popularizing private security, he focused primarily on crime prevention and investigation. During the American Civil War (1861–65; war in the United States between the Union [North], who was opposed to slavery, and the Confederacy [South], who was in favor of slavery), Pinkerton organized the first government-authorized secret service agency in American history.

The Pinkerton National Detective Agency was among the first private detective agencies in the world. (A detective is a police officer or investigator who investigates crimes and obtains evidence or information.) Allan Pinkerton introduced a number of innovative tools and methods to investigating criminal activity. Dubbed "The Pinks" (short for Pinkerton), his agency handled much of America's criminal investigation before the creation of the Federal Bureau of Investigation (FBI) and other modern police organizations.

Allan Pinkerton. *(The Library of Congress)*

A new life

Allan Pinkerton was born in Glasgow, Scotland, to Isabella McQueen and William Pinkerton, a police sergeant killed in the line of duty when Allan was a child. He apprenticed to a cooper, or barrel maker, in 1831 at the age of twelve and became active in a workers' protest movement as a young man. The "People's Charter," dubbed the "Chartists," was a revolt by the workingmen of the British Isles against the political power of their wealthy landlords. Most used peaceful methods of protest but there was a faction of the Chartist movement that used physical rebellion and rioting for political reform. After a Chartist physical altercation with the authorities in 1842, Allan Pinkerton's name appeared in the royal warrants for arrest. He fled the country with his new bride, Joan Carfrae.

The couple arrived in the United States and made their home in Dundee, Illinois, a small town settled by Scots just forty miles north of Chicago. Pinkerton advertised himself as the "Only and Original Cooper of Dundee" and soon had a prosperous business. He and Joan started a family in 1846, with three of their children surviving to adulthood.

Creates detective business

While searching for wood to make his barrels, Pinkerton accidentally discovered a counterfeit camp headquarters on an island in the middle of a lake, and quickly arranged for the arrest of the criminals. (Counterfeiting is making a copy of something in order to deceive, and around this time it was so widespread that it was affecting both the local and national economy.) He became a local hero and was sworn in as a deputy sheriff of Kane County, Illinois, in 1846. By 1850 the family moved to Chicago where Pinkerton worked for the local and federal government. The city was booming, with both business and crime flourishing.

When the Cook County police force was reorganized, Pinkerton was appointed their first, and only, detective. He became known to respectable citizens and criminals alike because of the number of arrests he made.

Pinkerton's reputation led to an appointment as special agent for the U.S. Post Office Department investigating fraud, extortion, and blackmail. With his detective work increasing and his own family growing, Pinkerton left the force to organize his own agency, the Pinkerton National Detective Agency. His methods focused more on preventing crime rather than responding to it. Within a few years he had eight additional employees.

In the early nineteenth century policing was organized on a county basis. Jurisdictions (areas over which law agencies had authority) did not extend beyond the frontiers of each individual state. At the same time, railroads were rapidly developing and criminals were able to roam vast areas of the country evading law enforcement. The railroads were increasingly vulnerable to the threat of violence towards trains and passengers, as well as their bridges, tracks, and terminals.

Unlike regular law enforcement, private detectives were able to cross state lines to pursue offenders. By organizing an agency whose operatives could work around boundaries, Pinkerton filled a large gap in law enforcement. Railroads hired Pinkerton to protect their companies from train robbers as well as from dishonest employees who collected fares and freight for their own purposes.

Setting up a spy system (or "testing program" as Pinkerton called it), allowed Pinkerton or one of his agents to board a train posing as a passenger and spy on its workers. For rail companies, such practices gave them control and accountability; for workers, the spying represented deception and mistrust. As Pinkerton's testing program expanded so did the anger of railway workers who organized labor unions to protect themselves.

Allan Pinkerton, left, standing with President Abraham Lincoln, center. Lincoln became a supporter of Pinkerton and his detective agency after Pinkerton uncovered and thus prevented an assassination plot against the president. *(The Library of Congress)*

America's Scotland Yard

While working for the Illinois Central Railroad, Pinkerton became acquainted with the firm's young attorney, Abraham Lincoln (1809–1865; served 1861–65). When Lincoln became president-elect in 1861, Pinkerton uncovered a plot to assassinate him when his train stopped at Baltimore on its way to Washington, D.C., for the inauguration. Pinkerton approached Lincoln's aides and personally arranged to bring the presidential party secretly to the capital by way of Maryland.

The Pinkerton National Detective Agency's capture record of criminals filled the newspapers and made Allan Pinkerton

The Molly Maguires

The year Allan Pinkerton left Scotland was the same year a secret society called the Molly Maguires was being organized in Ireland. Composed of laborers, it was formed to protect the peasantry from abuse by agents of wealthy landlords. They were known to use violence and sabotage. The name Molly Maguires came from their use of women's clothing as a disguise when hiding from law enforcement.

When a similar group of Irishmen organized into a union in the coal-mining districts of Pennsylvania in 1854, the press and police applied the name Molly Maguires to the American miners. Although no connection existed between the two societies, calling anyone who was for unions a "Molly" labeled them as a lawless element. As a result, uprisings were briefly subdued in the workplace. By 1875, however, the society had become a fraternity used to dominate miners' organizations and intimidate owners.

Ultimately, their activity led to a forced general strike. Contracted killings regularly occurred in order to rid the region of any mine superintendents, bosses, and police who opposed members of the order. As-

an internationally famous private detective. English journalists referred to the agency as "America's Scotland Yard" named after their own famous public detective agency. Pinkerton's protective methods were so successful that many criminals hesitated to rob a company that had been placed in the care of The Pinks. This reputation led to increased business for the agency and its chief, known as "the Principal."

When the American Civil War broke out Pinkerton was appointed head of the first secret service in America. He used his spy system to gather intelligence from his base in Virginia under the pseudonym (a made-up name) Major E. J. Allen. His operatives provided information to Washington from behind enemy lines in the South and also detected counterespionage activities treasonable to the Union in the North.

Pinkerton was a committed abolitionist (one who opposes slavery) who considered slavery to be a terrible crime that had to be eliminated, though he stopped short of an armed rebellion that was advocated and later carried out by abolitionist and friend John Brown (1800–1859). Because of the Fugitive Slave Law that required runaway slaves be returned to their

sassins were always brought in from another district, so they would not be recognized. This pattern made it difficult to produce a case against the Molly Maguires. Originally intended to improve working conditions and secure fair wages, the union was soon responsible for blowing up mines, wrecking trains, setting fires, and looting company stores, in addition to murder.

After repeated attempts to bring the offenders to justice failed, the Philadelphia and Reading Coal and Iron Company brought in Pinkerton. The agency decided to use an undercover agent, and in the fall of 1873 operative James McParland was assigned to infiltrate the Mollys. Posing as James McKenna, a fugitive from a murder charge in Buffalo, McParland soon made his mark in the Irish community of the coalfields.

By the spring of 1874 McParland was inducted into the secret society and continued sending reports to the Pinkerton office about labor conditions in the field for another year. McParland needed to gather enough evidence of crimes committed to stand up in a court of law. His work ultimately resulted in the conviction and execution of several union leaders, although his report charged that the company was largely responsible for the explosive situation in the coal-mining districts.

masters, Pinkerton operated on two sides of the law in what he considered a clear-cut issue.

When Pinkerton first settled in the United States his cooperage in Dundee became a station on the Underground Railroad. It provided aid to slaves escaping from the South to Canada. Besides food, shelter, and clothing, Pinkerton taught them barrel making and carpentry skills whenever possible so they could earn a living as free men. Pinkerton's participation increased in Chicago where his friend, John Brown, and others would protect liberated slaves before they boarded lake steamers for Canada.

Private eye

Pinkerton was assigned by Lincoln to spy on Confederate (Southern) troops during the war, and in 1865, Pinkerton returned from his service and resumed leadership of his agency. The agency profited from the war but saw opportunities multiply in peacetime. He opened branches in New York City and Philadelphia while expanding the agency's role internationally. Under extradition treaties (international agreements to return wanted criminals) he returned criminals who fled their countries to avoid prosecution. The Pinkerton agency was well known for its pursuit of the Jessie James gang (notorious bank and train robbers) and other infamous criminals from 1867 through 1875.

The agency was also assuming another new role, policing labor disputes between management and the new unions forming in America. As a new company Pinkerton began by policing railroads, but over the next two decades he became involved in policing labor union strikes for industry. The Pinks intervened in some seventy strikes, often with violent consequences and bad publicity. Pinkerton was accused of being antiunion. The agency had a leading role in breaking up the Molly Maguires, an often violent laborers group (see sidebar).

Pinkerton worked hard to promote the role of the detective as a high and honorable calling. He wrote numerous books on detection that gave accounts of skilled investigators who were pure and above reproach. His company's advertising stated that he would only take on such business as was strictly legitimate and that would bring criminals to justice. A fee structure was established and work for posted rewards was forbidden. Employees followed a code of conduct for habits and dress that were meant to mirror the respectable businesses they served.

On the facade (outside front wall) of his three-story Chicago headquarters was the company slogan, "We Never Sleep." Above the words was a wide-awake human eye in black and white. The trademark became known as "The Eye." Over time the general public called private detectives "private eyes." Allan Pinkerton hired the first female detective in America. He also called his employees "operatives" as an early means of separating them from corrupt practices associated with other detectives.

Pinkerton pioneered the use of wanted posters of the criminals his agency was seeking. The posters included names, aliases, physical features, and reward information along with photographs. Pinkerton worked in the field himself throughout his career, often in disguise. He maintained a large collection of costumes and wigs in his office to assume the appearance of any occupation that might be needed in a case.

Pinkerton suffered a paralyzing stroke in 1868 and withdrew from daily operations at the agency. He continued to write his memoirs, although a major fire in Chicago in 1871 destroyed much of the city's business district and burned most of his records. Pinkerton died in 1884 and was buried in the family plot at Graceland Cemetery, Chicago. His sons, William and Robert, took over and expanded the agency after his death. The trademark name *Pinkerton* was still in use in the early twenty-first century as a brand name for security services.

For More Information

Books

Lavine, Sigmund A. *Allan Pinkerton: America's First Private Eye.* New York: Dodd, Mead & Company, 1963.

Levinson, David, ed. *Encyclopedia of Crime and Punishment.* Thousand Oaks, CA: Sage Publications, 2002.

Mackay, James. *Allan Pinkerton: The First Private Eye.* New York: John Wiley & Sons, Inc., 1996.

Web Sites

"The Molly Maguires." *Providence College.* http://www.providence.edu/polisci/students/molly_maguires/ (accessed on August 15, 2004).

"Pinkerton Detective Agency." *The National Archives Learning Curve.* http://www.spartacus.schoolnet.co.uk/USApinkertonD.htm (accessed on August 15, 2004).

Scottsboro Boys

Accused rapists

In 1931 the United States was in the second year of the Great Depression (1929–41; the period, following the stock market crash in 1929, of depressed world economies and high unemployment). On March 25 in Chattanooga, Tennessee, a Southern Railroad freight train eased out of the station headed west. Dozens of people, men and women, black and white, jumped on board for a free ride. For nine young black men from the South, the ride would change their lives forever.

Olen Montgomery, Clarence Norris, Haywood Patterson, Ozie Powell, Willie Roberson, Charles Weems, Eugene Williams, Andy Wright, and Roy Wright ranged in age from twelve to twenty years. Five were from Georgia and four were teenagers from Tennessee. They had hopped the train in search of government work in Memphis, Tennessee. All nine were arrested for the alleged rape of two white women on the freight train. They were taken to jail in nearby Scottsboro, Alabama.

Most of the young men spent the next two decades in courtrooms and prisons and would become known as the Scottsboro Boys. Their case would change U.S. criminal law

The nine men accused of rape in what became known as the Scottsboro case shortly after their arrest in 1931. *(© Bettmann/Corbis)*

and result in two important Supreme Court decisions affecting criminal procedure.

A long ride

It was early spring in 1931 and the Southern Railroad freight train had just crossed the border into Alabama. It stopped for water in Stevenson where a fight broke out between two groups of young men who were riding the train. One group was black and one was white. The outnumbered white teenagers either jumped or were thrown from the train as it pulled out of the station.

Some of the white youths sought revenge and told the Stevenson train master about the rape of two white women who were still on the train. The train master telegraphed ahead to have the train stopped at the next station. Law enforcement officers boarded the forty-two-car train at Paint Rock, Alabama, and arrested every black youth they could find. They were loaded on a flatbed truck and taken to the jail in Scottsboro, Alabama.

That night word spread of the alleged crime. Governor B. M. Miller called out the National Guard to protect the prison where the youths were held. The next day they were taken by the state militia to Gadsden, Alabama, for safekeeping. Many local newspapers had already run condemning headlines before the case even went to trial.

The accusers

The alleged rape victims in the Scottsboro case were Victoria Price and Ruby Bates. Both were from poor families who lived in a racially mixed section of town in Huntsville, Alabama. Twenty-one-year-old Victoria and the teenaged Ruby were mill workers. Both were familiar with "hoboing," or catching rides on freight trains. The women hopped the train from Huntsville to Chattanooga on March 24 looking for work. They were returning on March 25 when they were caught in the police roundup in Paint Rock, Alabama.

When questioned by police they said they had been beaten and raped by a gang of black men carrying pistols and knives. Price identified six young men who were being held at the jail. The police assumed the other three in custody had attacked Bates.

Scottsboro physician Dr. R. R. Bridges examined Price and Bates less than two hours after the alleged assault had occurred. He found little evidence to support their contention of being victims of a violent attack. Bridges reported no lacerations or blood, no serious bruising or head injuries, and described the women as calm and composed during the examination. Victoria Price, however, testified that they had been crying and in a state of shock.

Legal wrangling

On March 31 all nine of the Scottsboro Boys were indicted for rape. The defense team consisted of an unpaid and un-

Samuel Leibowitz

Samuel Leibowitz (1893–1978) was a noted New York attorney who represented the Scottsboro Boys after their initial 1931 trial. Leibowitz represented seventy-eight persons charged with first-degree murder in his fifteen-year career as a criminal defense attorney. His record showed seventy-seven acquittals, one hung jury, and no convictions. In the courtroom, Leibowitz had a compelling personality to accompany his detailed preparation and knowledge of the law.

Leibowitz read the court records of the first Scottsboro trial after receiving a call from the International Labor Defense (ILD). The ILD asked him to defend the Scottsboro Boys in their second trial. It was the medical testimony of Dr. R. R. Bridges saying that the alleged victims in the case had not been beaten or raped that convinced him of the boys' innocence, and he accepted the ILD's offer.

Many questioned Leibowitz's decision to take such a difficult case. He was a mainstream Democrat who had not been associated with racial causes. In this case, however, Leibowitz was serious in his quest for justice. He worked for several years without pay or reimbursement from his clients. His efforts won him the respect and gratitude of the Scottsboro Boys as well as several in the black community.

Leibowitz soon became the target of death threats in Alabama. He was assigned five uniformed members of the National Guard to protect him. Because of the nature

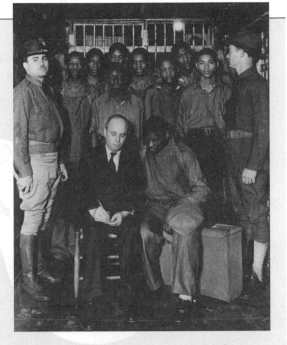

Attorney Sam Leibowitz meeting with his clients, the Scottsboro boys. *(© Bettmann/Corbis)*

of the case, the governor made 150 more guardsmen available to defend against a possible lynch mob. Following several convictions in the marathon Scottsboro case, Leibowitz and the ILD ended up battling for control of the case. The animosity grew when two ILD attorneys were charged with attempting to bribe Victoria Price, who hinted that money could help change her story.

Leibowitz eventually took the Scottsboro Case to the U.S. Supreme Court and won the decision in *Norris v. Alabama.* The Supreme Court reversed the convictions of the lower courts when it was shown that blacks were illegally excluded from Alabama juries.

prepared Chattanooga real estate attorney and a seventy-year-old local attorney who had not tried a case in decades. The prosecution broke the trials down into groups of two or three defendants each and began deliberations on April 6. All four trials were completed in three days. Eight of the boys were sentenced to death by electric chair. Twelve-year-old Roy Wright received a mistrial when eleven of the jurors wanted the death penalty, though the prosecution had specifically requested life imprisonment due to his age.

Several hours after the guilty sentences were handed down the International Labor Defense (ILD) wired Governor Miller demanding a stay (delay) of execution. The ILD was the legal arm of the American Communist Party, a radical political group trying to gain the support of oppressed minorities. The ILD moved aggressively to represent the case when the National Association for the Advancement of Colored People (NAACP) hesitated to take it due to the nature of the charges. The ILD pronounced the case a murderous frame-up and an example of the oppression of blacks in the United States.

When the ILD took over the defense they sought new trials by appealing the initial verdicts. They also gave the case international publicity. In January 1932 the Alabama Supreme Court affirmed all but one of the convictions and death sentences. They ruled that Eugene Williams, aged thirteen, should not have been tried as an adult. The ILD appealed to the U.S. Supreme Court.

In October 1932 the convictions were overturned in the landmark case of *Powell v. Alabama*. The Court ruled that Alabama denied the right of the defendants to competent legal counsel under the Fourteenth Amendment's due process clause, which ensured fair treatment in the legal system and the right to a fair and public trial. The Scottsboro Boys were granted new trials.

Second chances

For the second trials, the ILD called in renowned New York attorney Samuel Leibowitz (see sidebar) for the defense. The Scottsboro Boys spent the next two years in prison in Decatur, Alabama, awaiting their March 1933 trial date. Haywood Patterson's case was separated from the other defendants and came before Judge James Horton on March 28.

A large crowd of demonstrators protesting the Scottsboro jury's condemnation of Haywood Patterson. *(© Underwood & Underwood/Corbis)*

The trial took a dramatic turn when Ruby Bates appeared for the defense to reverse her testimony from the first trial. She testified that she and Victoria Price had made up the rape story to avoid arrest themselves. They had feared possible charges of vagrancy or violation of the Mann Act (crossing state lines for immoral purposes). Bates said Price had encouraged her to make false accusations to direct attention away from their situation. Price, however, maintained her original testimony. Patterson was convicted and sentenced to die in the electric chair.

Since the arrest of the Scottsboro Boys in 1931, public support had been growing throughout Alabama, the United

States, and around the world. Demonstrations calling for the release of the Scottsboro Boys occurred outside U.S. embassies throughout Europe. On May 1, 1931, some 300,000 black and white workers in 110 American cities protested the Scottsboro convictions in May Day celebrations. On May 5, 1933, a crowd marched on Washington, D.C., carrying a petition signed by 200,000 supporters demanding freedom for the Scottsboro Boys.

Continuing the good fight

Judge Norton decided justice had been denied to Haywood Patterson and granted a motion for a new trial. Horton wrote a lengthy opinion reviewing the case and concluded the jury's conviction was not justified by the evidence. For his efforts, he lost reelection as a judge and his political career came to an end. In December 1933, the State of Alabama tried Patterson for the third time and once again sentenced him to die. Clarence Norris was put on trial for the second time and was similarly convicted and sentenced to die.

Leibowitz, stunned by the guilty verdicts, vowed to defend the Boys to the end. He appealed both cases unsuccessfully to the Alabama Supreme Court. Leibowitz then appealed to the U.S. Supreme Court. The Court granted reviews of both cases in January 1935. Later that April, in a landmark decision, the Supreme Court reversed both convictions in *Norris v. Alabama*. The Court ruled on the grounds that blacks had been systematically excluded from serving on grand juries and trial juries. The defendants were not being judged by their peers as required by law.

The aftermath

Haywood Patterson was tried yet again in January 1936 and once again convicted. This time he received a sentence of seventy-five years imprisonment. It was the first time in Alabama history that a black man convicted of raping a white woman had not been sentenced to death.

By the summer of 1937, after numerous trials, appeals, and years in prison the case of the Scottsboro Boys was reaching the end. Seven of the nine Scottsboro Boys had been held in jail for over six years without a trial. On July 12 Clarence Norris began his third trial, which ended with a conviction and a death sentence. Andrew Wright was convicted on July 22. He received a sentence of ninety-nine years. Charles Weems received a seventy-five year sentence two days later.

In a surprise move the State of Alabama dropped charges and announced the freedom of Olen Montgomery, Willie Roberson, Eugene Williams, and Roy Wright. Ozie Powell had his charges dropped when he pled guilty to assault and received a twenty-year sentence. The five Scottsboro defendants jailed remained in prison while demonstrations for their freedom continued until 1942. By that time America became preoccupied with World War II (1939–45).

Either by parole or escape, all of the Scottsboro Boys eventually left Alabama but found limited success in life. Clarence Norris was the only Scottsboro defendant who lived to see an official pardon by the State of Alabama in 1976.

For More Information

Books

Carter, Dan T. *Scottsboro: A Tragedy of the American South.* Baton Rouge, LA: Louisiana State University Press, 1969.

Goodman, James. *Stories of Scottsboro.* New York: Pantheon Books, 1994.

Patterson, Haywood, and Earl Conrad. *Scottsboro Boy.* Garden City, NY: Doubleday & Company, Inc., 1950.

Web Sites

"Scottsboro: An American Tragedy." *PBS Online.* http://www.pbs.org/ wgbh/amex/scottsboro/index.html (accessed on August 15, 2004).

"Scottsboro Boys." *Decatur/Morgan County Convention & Visitors Bureau.* http://www.decaturcvb.org/Pages/Press/scotboy.html (accessed on August 15, 2004).

Sam Sheppard

Born December 23, 1923 (Cleveland, Ohio)
Died April 6, 1970 (Columbus, Ohio)

Accused murderer, physician

"I couldn't kill a squirrel or a rabbit much less someone I loved."

In 1954 Dr. Sam Sheppard was accused of the brutal murder of his wife Marilyn at their home in Cleveland, Ohio. Before the sensational Sheppard criminal case was over, a landmark Supreme Court ruling would be handed down on the widely debated conflict between freedom of the press and a defendant's right to a fair trial. The decision set specific guidelines for criminal trial court judges to follow in an effort to protect jurors from too much publicity.

American criminal law operates on the assumption that someone is innocent until proven guilty in a court of law. The news media, however, assumed the role of judge and jury during the investigation and subsequent trial of Dr. Sam Sheppard in 1954. He was essentially condemned in the court of public opinion before he went to trial. A review by the Supreme Court in 1966 ruled that Sheppard did not receive a fail trial and he was ultimately cleared of the crime. His story inspired a highly popular television series and a Hollywood movie, both known as *The Fugitive.*

Dr. Sam Sheppard. *(AP/Wide World Photos)*

A promising future

Samuel Holmes Sheppard was the third son born to Dr. Richard and Ethel Sheppard. His father founded Bay View Hospital, an osteopathic (medical treatment of bones and muscle) facility located in an elite lakefront suburb on Cleveland's west side. Samuel graduated from Cleveland Heights High School the year after his high school sweetheart, Marilyn Reese. They were married in Hollywood, California, in 1945, while Samuel attended the Los Angeles College of Osteopathic Physicians and Surgeons.

In 1947 Samuel and Marilyn had a son and named him Sam. After receiving his medical degree, Samuel joined his father and two elder brothers, Richard and Stephen, in business. Sheppard moved his young family back to Bay Village, Ohio, and purchased a home on the shore of Lake Erie.

Sheppard took up surgical residence at Bay View Hospital, where he was called Dr. Sam to distinguish him from the other Dr. Sheppards. The family of physicians worked together and prospered at the hospital, the town's largest employer, as well as in their private practice in the nearby suburb of Fairview Park. For the next few years Dr. Sam was on emergency medical call more than one third of his evenings, just as he was on the holiday weekend of July 4, 1954.

Independence Day

On July 3, Sam Sheppard returned home from an emergency call to enjoy a late dinner with his wife and several guests before falling asleep on the couch in the living room. Marilyn, who was four months pregnant, went upstairs to bed around midnight after saying goodbye to their guests. Four hours later, in the early morning hours of July 4, Marilyn Sheppard was beaten to death while her husband slept downstairs.

Sam heard Marilyn calling him and ran upstairs to the dimly lit room where he saw a bushy-haired form in light clothing standing next to his wife's bed. He wrestled with the intruder before being knocked unconscious. When Sam awoke he found his wife dead and then went to his seven-year-old son's room to find him sleeping soundly. Sheppard went downstairs when he heard noises and chased the killer down to the lakefront before being knocked out a second time. When Sam stumbled back to his home he called for help and the Bay Village police responded.

The Bay Village police department had never investigated a murder in their quiet community. They called in the Cleveland police as well as the county coroner to help. The coroner arrived before 8:00 A.M. and cleared the home of friends and neighbors before securing the crime scene. Early in its investigation the police concluded the murderer had been very familiar with Sheppard's property and home.

By mid-afternoon the coroner and one of the detectives accused Sheppard of murdering his wife and began searching for his motive. Although Sheppard had no history of violent behavior and was well-liked in his community, officials focused their investigation on him from the beginning.

The morning after Marilyn Sheppard died all three Cleveland newspapers published headlines about the murder. By mid-morning, lines of cars drove slowly past the Sheppard home with passengers leaning out of windows to snap photographs. Some parked their vehicles and walked into the yard for a closer look. For the next month the Sheppard murder case was closely followed with daily news reports that started out sympathetic to Dr. Sam but evolved into accusations.

By the end of July front page editorials claimed investigators were inept and that Sheppard's social standing was shielding him from justice. He was arrested on murder charges the evening of July 30 and taken to Bay Village City Hall. Hundreds of people, including newscasters, photographers, and reporters, were there awaiting his arrival.

Marilyn Sheppard, the murdered wife of Dr. Sam Sheppard. Dr. Sheppard was wrongly convicted of her death but later released. *(AP/Wide World Photos)*

Character assassination

Sheppard's trial was set to begin October 18 with Sheppard maintaining his story that he had confronted and fought the attacker. Extensive pretrial publicity across the country made the case so notorious that it resulted in a frenzied atmosphere when the trial date finally arrived. Outside the courthouse, on the sidewalks and steps, the national media waited to take pictures of Sheppard and other trial participants.

Inside the courtroom the judge allowed space to be reserved for television and newspaper reporters. Broadcasting facilities for radio were set up at the courthouse so newscasts could be made daily throughout the trial. Records of the day's

F. Lee Bailey

F. Lee Bailey was a recent graduate of Boston University Law School and an aspiring criminal attorney when he was introduced to the Sheppard case in the early 1960s. He began the appeals process for Sam Sheppard arguing that his trial had been unfair and so was his continued prison sentence. Bailey filed the writ (written request) in Ohio's southern federal district in 1963 so it would be considered by U.S. District Judge Carl Weinman of Dayton.

Weinman ruled in Sheppard's favor but a federal court of appeals overturned the decision by a vote of two to one. Failing on a second plea to the same court, Bailey filed a petition with the U.S. Supreme Court. The Court was itself already focusing on granting defendants better legal standing in the criminal justice system. In February 1966, Bailey successfully presented his case. The Supreme Court ruled that Sam Sheppard did not receive a fair trial due to publicity before and during the trial that unfairly influenced or prejudiced the jury.

Cleveland authorities could not recharge Sheppard with first-degree murder under the double jeopardy prohibition in the Constitution. Double jeopardy means a person cannot be tried twice for the same crime. Instead they brought second-degree murder charges against him. Sheppard found himself, once again, in court. Bailey

proceedings in court were printed word-for-word by newspapers, accompanied by photographs of the participants and exhibits introduced at trial. The new medium of television made the media exposure unprecedented in American history.

On the first day of the trial, the jury viewed the scene of the murder. One representative of the news media was permitted to accompany the jury while they inspected the Sheppard home. Hundreds more reporters, cameramen, and onlookers waited outside. On December 17 the case was submitted to the jury for deliberation. They returned four days later with a guilty verdict. Sheppard was convicted of murder and sentenced to life in prison. The *Cleveland Press* sold thirty thousand extra copies of their newspaper on the night of the verdict.

An acquittal

Sheppard served ten years in the Ohio Penitentiary in Columbus for the murder of his wife before the U.S. Supreme

Attorney F. Lee Bailey. *(The Library of Congress)*

provided an aggressive defense beginning on November 1, 1966. It ended with a not-guilty verdict after only eighteen days of testimony. Bailey's strategy was to raise reasonable doubt in the jurors' minds and propose other suspects in the murder case.

Over his long career Bailey used his skills as a criminal defense attorney to defend several high profile cases including the Albert DeSalvo (1931–1973; also known as the "Boston Strangler"), Patty Hearst (1954–), and O.J. Simpson (1947–). Bailey was a master at cross-examination and was among the first to use a jury consultant to help him select jurors at trial. He was known to hold press conferences to discuss the progress of his cases, which added to his notoriety.

Court ruled that the media had corrupted the original trial. A second trial in 1966 included pioneering work in crime scene investigation and blood evidence to prove Sheppard could not have killed Marilyn. Attorney F. Lee Bailey (1933–; see sidebar) won Sheppard's acquittal in 1967. A hostile press, however, continued to track Sheppard throughout his remaining years.

Sheppard's life became the inspiration for a popular television program called *The Fugitive.* In the television version, and a later movie version, the innocent doctor is accused of murdering his wife but escapes from prison and spends years on the run in search of the real killer. Both fictional and real life stories ended with the acquittal of the husband. Although in the film version the killer is apprehended, in the real-life Sheppard case the killer was never brought to justice.

Sheppard was finally a free man but he had lost his wife, and his son had been raised by his brother for over a decade. He tried to return to medicine in Ohio in 1968 but his skills had seriously deteriorated while he was in prison. The board at Youngstown Osteopathic Hospital restored Sheppard's surgical privileges but he was dismissed following several malpractice lawsuits. Dr. Sam Sheppard died of liver failure in 1970 at the age of forty-six.

For More Information

Books

Cooper, Cynthia L., and Sam Reese Sheppard. *Mockery of Justice: The True Story of the Sheppard Murder Case.* Boston, MA: Northeastern University Press, 1995.

Hixson, Walter L. *Murder, Culture, and Injustice: Four Sensational Cases in American History.* Akron, OH: University of Akron Press, 2001.

Neff, James. *The Wrong Man.* New York: Random House, 2001.

Web Sites

"F. Lee Bailey Biography." *University of Missouri.* http://www.law.umkc.edu/faculty/projects/ftrials/Simpson/Bailey.htm (accessed on August 15, 2004).

Sheppard v. Maxwell: U.S. Supreme Court. Sam Reese Sheppard: Seeking the Truth. http://www.samreesesheppard.org/shepvsmax.html (accessed on August 15, 2004).

Sally Stanford

Born May 5, 1903 (Baker City, Oregon)
Died February 1, 1982 (Greenbrae, California)

San Francisco madam

Sally Stanford was a bootlegger of illegal liquor during Prohibition in the 1930s before becoming a famous San Francisco madam during the 1930s and 1940s. A madam is a woman who manages a house of prostitution, also known as a brothel. Stanford supplied prostitutes to male customers and collected a percentage of the prostitute's fee. Experiencing financial success, Stanford opened brothels in the elite sections of San Francisco, catering to wealthy and influential men from around the world. Stanford eventually left prostitution to avoid prosecution and went into legitimate business. She was eventually elected mayor of Sausalito, California, and was the subject of a movie.

"Personally, I never met a white slave in my life. . . . If captive females were sold, drugged, and slugged into prostitution, I never knew [of] a case."

Poor beginnings

Sally Stanford, named Marcia Busby at birth, was the second of six children born to a poor family in Baker, Oregon. Her mother was an English teacher and her father an unsuccessful farmer. Marcia had an older sister and a younger brother. The family commonly called her Marcy while growing up. Developers built a golf course in Baker, and at just

Vices or Crimes, or Both

A longstanding debate among criminologists concerns how to treat certain crimes. Some argue activities such as gambling, drug use, pornography, and prostitution should simply be considered social "vices" (immoral actions) and not crimes. While they may be morally offensive, they should not be the subject of criminal laws. These activities are often called "victimless crimes" because they usually involve an agreed upon exchange of goods and services between adults. Some believe if these vices are decriminalized, it would decrease government involvement in people's lives and reduce criminal caseloads in court.

Opponents to decriminalizing vice crimes argue that these crimes impose financial and social costs on individuals and society in general. As a result, they should not be considered victimless. They point out that compulsive gamblers and drug addicts are often driven to steal in order to support their expensive habits. The resulting victims endure the costs of replacing damaged or stolen property as well as increasing costs of protection and insurance.

In regard to prostitution, it affects women, children, and minorities more so than other groups and places them at risk of assault and health dangers. Individuals, and society as a whole, face increased costs for medical treatment and the spread of disease both nationally and internationally. In

seven years old, Marcy caddied for the golfers earning fifteen cents a round to help support the family.

Marcy's education stopped at the third grade when her father moved the family to Sunnyslope, a town located five miles outside of Baker on the old Oregon Trail. (The Oregon Trail was opened in 1842. It was a trail from the Middle West to what is now western Oregon taken by thousands of migrants.) From there the family would move often between Oregon and California through the following years.

An aunt soon took Marcy in but died when Marcy was a young teenager. She was next sent to help her uncle and grandparents in Santa Paula, California. There she met a young fellow named LeRoy Snyder. They both lied about their age to marry. The marriage was annulled (legally ended) nine days later and Marcy returned to Oregon, where she went to work as a server in a restaurant and met another young man.

addition, prostitution is seen as one of society's clearest expressions of the sexual domination of men over women and young people.

In 1873 Congress took a major step in criminalizing vice by the passage of the Comstock Law. The act targeted what it considered obscene literature, sought to restrict the flow of birth control information, and was used to fight abortion. In 1910 at a peak in vice-fighting in the United States, Congress passed the Mann Act. The act targeted what it termed "white slavery," or forced prostitution. The law assumed that all women in prostitution were involved against their will.

Congress concluded that women and girls in prostitution had become indentured sex slaves, forced into prostitution for someone else's financial gain because of the debts they owed. Specifically, the act made it a federal crime to transport women over state lines for immoral or sexual purposes. In the first five years of the act, over one thousand defendants were found guilty of Mann Act violations. Most offenders were male, but a study found some 160 women were convicted in one ten-year period beginning in the late 1920s.

In later times, fear rose of drug-addicted prostitutes becoming slaves, kept in houses and given drugs in exchange for sex with the dealers and their clients. In 1986 Congress amended the act to include any sexual activity that could be considered a criminal offense.

The two were caught passing bad checks and Marcy ended up at the Oregon State Penitentiary in Salem.

By this time Prohibition (1919–33; law making alcohol illegal) was just beginning. The Prohibition laws banned the sale, possession, and production of alcoholic beverages. While in the Oregon prison Marcy learned about bootlegging, or supplying illegal alcohol to willing customers, from other inmates. She was just eighteen years old when she was released from prison. She moved to Ventura, California, and set up her own bootlegging business.

Using the name Marcia Wells, she bought a white Packard automobile and purchased an old Spanish house overlooking the Pacific Ocean. Her bootlegging operation was booming when she met Ernest Spagnoli, an attorney from San Francisco, California. At the age of twenty, Marcia married Spagnoli and moved to San Francisco. The couple soon divorced, but not before they had adopted a baby boy. With money left over from her bootlegging, Marcia bought a little hotel at 693 O'Farrell Street in 1929 and began operating a brothel.

San Francisco Madam

Police began investigating Marcia's business in the early 1930s. Because of her criminal record in Oregon, she feared she might end up in prison again. As a precaution, she sent her adopted baby to live with her mother in Oregon. As she expected, authorities charged her with operating a house of prostitution. Marcia was acquitted but found she was stuck with the label "madam" by the news media. She decided to make it official and go into the business in a bigger way.

Marcia's first order of business was to create a new name in order to avoid embarrassing her former attorney husband with whom she remained friends. One weekend the two local universities, the University of California and Stanford University, played a football game against each other. After seeing the resulting newspaper headlines about Stanford beating California and having just won her trial against the state, she decided Stanford would be a good fit for her new surname. Then, while dining out, a band played a popular tune, "I Wonder What's Become of Sally?" and Sally Stanford was born.

Stanford set up a business at 610 Leavenworth Street in San Francisco. She hired a group of professional prostitutes, created an inviting atmosphere, and hung up a sign advertising "Rooms." San Francisco had many establishments for gambling, drinking, and prostitution at the time but Stanford's business flourished. She attracted a wealthy clientele from the city's high-society, including government officials. Stanford established several more houses and married once again, this time to a man named Lou Rapp.

Stanford kept busy throughout the 1930s despite the Great Depression (1929–41) and the growing threat of the United States entering World War II (1939–45; war in which Great Britain, France, the Soviet Union, the United States, and their allied forces defeated Germany, Italy, and Japan). The Great Depression was a major economic crisis lasting from 1929 to 1941 leading to massive unemployment and widespread hunger. It was also a time of numerous official investigations

High-end prostitutes being arrested in 1943 after being rounded up on vice charges. *(© Bettmann/Corbis)*

into corruption spreading throughout the country. Prostitution was often included because of its ties to organized crime and white slavery (see sidebar).

The Bureau of Internal Revenue began a grand jury investigation when a San Francisco police captain was suspected of bribery and tax evasion. The bureau hired a former Federal Bureau of Investigation (FBI) agent named Edwin Atherton to conduct a thorough search into prostitution in the city. The Atherton Report resulted in a series of indictments (formal charges). Feeling increasingly uncomfortable with the investigations, Sally Stanford decided it was time to look for a new location for her business enterprise.

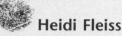

Heidi Fleiss

Sally Stanford was not the last of the famous California madams of the twentieth century. In the 1980s Heidi Fleiss (1966–) became known as the "Hollywood Madam." Fleiss provided prostitutes to the rich and famous in Hollywood and beyond. Fleiss learned her trade while working for Elizabeth Adams, known as the infamous Madam Alex. Adams ran the most prosperous prostitution service in Los Angeles.

In 1986 Fleiss decided to go into business on her own. At the age of twenty, with her earnings from Adams, Fleiss purchased a home in the Benedict Canyon section of Los Angeles. She hired beautiful young women from the area's population of aspiring actresses, university students, and businesswomen. Within months she had cornered the high-end prostitution market and was earning millions of dollars.

In June 1993 law enforcement closed in and ended Fleiss's lucrative operation. She was arraigned in August and entered a plea of not guilty. Fleiss agreed to a plea bargain (pleading guilty to a lesser charge so that prosecution drops more serious charge) and was convicted on three counts of pandering (acquiring prostitutes) in charges filed against her by the state of California. Her legal troubles, however, were not over. In 1995 a federal jury convicted Fleiss on eight

Hollywood Madam Heidi Fleiss. *(AP/Wide World Photos)*

counts of conspiracy, tax evasion, and money laundering. Her father, Dr. Paul Fleiss, a Los Angeles pediatrician, received three years probation for his part in the conspiracy.

Heidi Fleiss received a total of three years in prison for the state and federal convictions as well as an additional three hundred hours of community service. Upon her release in September 1999, Fleiss engaged in legitimate business ventures and wrote a book appropriately titled *Pandering* that described her experiences.

A move to legitimacy

In 1941 Stanford moved her prostitution business to 1144 Pine Street. She remained there until November 1949 when a young woman under eighteen years of age was arrested for fighting on the street. She claimed she worked at Sally's place. As a result, authorities arrested Stanford and prosecuted her for contributing to the delinquency of a minor, a felony criminal charge. Much to her relief, she was once again acquitted, but it signaled the end of her days as a madam.

Stanford opened a restaurant called the "Valhalla" just across the Golden Gate Bridge north of San Francisco in the suburb of Sausalito. She also married a wealthy dealer in Oriental art. Becoming well established in the business community, Stanford served as vice president of the Chamber of Commerce and was a popular figure in the town's social circles. Stanford was elected mayor of Sausalito in 1976.

In 1966 Stanford published her autobiography, *The Lady of the House*. Hollywood actress Dyan Cannon (1937–) portrayed Stanford in a television movie version of the book. Through her life Stanford used over twenty names and was arrested seventeen times, but only convicted twice. She survived eleven heart attacks and colon cancer surgery. She died of heart failure in 1982.

For More Information

Books

Brock, Deborah R. *Making Work, Making Trouble: Prostitution as a Social Problem*. Toronto, Ontario: University of Toronto Press, 1998.

Flowers, R. Barri. *The Prostitution of Women and Girls*. Jefferson, NC: Mc-Farland & Company, Inc., Publishers, 1998.

Stanford, Sally. *The Lady of the House*. New York: G. P. Putnam's Sons, 1966.

Web Site

"Infamous Inmates: Sally Stanford, 1949." *San Francisco Sheriff's Department*. http://www.ci.sf.ca.us/site/sheriff_index.asp?id=25456 (accessed on August 15, 2004).

George Washington Walling

Born May 1, 1823 (New York)
Died December 31, 1891 (New York)

New York City police chief

"All the sneaks, hypocrites and higher grade of criminals . . . almost invariably lay claim to be adherents of the Republican Party . . . criminals of the lower order, those who rob by violence and brute force, lay claim . . . to . . . true Democratic principles."

George Washington Walling was the police chief of New York City from July 1874 until June 1885. Walling gained a reputation as a tough but fair and honest law officer during his decades on the force. He was elevated to the position of chief of police because of his personal heroics during the New York City Draft Riots of 1863 while serving as captain of the twentieth precinct on the lower West Side of the city. His able leadership helped restore order to a city in crisis during the American Civil War (1861–65; war in the United States between the Union [North], who was opposed to slavery, and the Confederacy [South], who was in favor of slavery). Throughout his law career Walling worked toward bringing professionalism to the New York police force by freeing it from connections to corrupt city politics. Professionalism in policing made giant strides in the later half of the nineteenth century due to the work of Walling and others.

To protect and serve

Walling was the son of Leonard Sr. and Catherine Aumack Walling. He joined the New York City police department at a time when badges were made of stamped copper. Since policemen wore civilian clothes while on duty, their only identification was their patrolman's badge. It earned the officers the nickname "coppers" which, over time, was shortened to "cops." During Walling's time on the force, police saw a steady trend toward increased professionalism, even in their dress. A uniform was eventually required, consisting of a blue coat with a velvet collar and nine black buttons. The black buttons were later replaced with brass ones. Each patrolman was supposed to wear gray trousers with a one-inch black stripe down the sides to complete the uniform.

The police force of New York City was largely made up of urban laboring classes who were largely Irish in the early 1800s. Corruption was extensive and well known to the public. An aspiring patrolman was required to pay a fee in order to receive an appointment from the New York City Common Council. By the mid-1800s gangs were a real problem in the city as they robbed and assaulted at will. The New York City Municipal Police District had thirty-two precincts when it was created in 1853. George Walling became captain of the twentieth precinct at that time.

When Walling took command of the twentieth precinct he found the district living in fear of a group of particularly violent thugs called the Honeymoon Gang. Because of political graft (politicians paid by criminals), arresting the criminals was useless because they were immediately released and the abuses quickly resumed. Walling took a different approach. He assembled his largest officers into a squad armed with wooden clubs to enforce the law in his precinct. Seeing that the policemen meant business, the Honeymoon Gang fled to other areas.

The mayor's office

In 1854 Fernando Wood (1812–1881) was elected mayor of New York City. During his first term of office conditions went from bad to worse because of his corrupt administration. In a rigged election in 1857, Wood won a second term in office and the state legislature stepped in. They shortened his term from two years to one and created a Metropolitan police force to replace Wood's corrupt Municipal police. A board of

An 1865 drawing of the Metropolitan police. George Walling was one of the lawmen who signed on with New York's Metropolitan police.
(© Corbis)

commissioners appointed by the governor replaced the Common Council to hire law enforcement agents. Wood contended the amending legislative act was unconstitutional and refused to step down even when faced with a Supreme Court order.

George Walling was one of the lawmen who signed on with the new state-created Metropolitan police. Fifteen other captains, along with hundreds of their patrolmen, elected to stay with Wood and the Municipal police. While the politicians sorted out the mess, New Yorkers were faced with rival patrolmen as both forces patrolled the city's precincts. Those arrested by one police force were often set free by aldermen (city councilmen) or magistrates (local judges) whose loyalties were with the opposite side. Gangs took advantage of the weakness in law enforcement and were soon joined by criminals from elsewhere.

Walling was personally assigned the task of arresting Mayor Wood. Armed with a warrant, he entered City Hall alone and was allowed to reach Wood's office. When Walling attempted to arrest Wood, he was thrown out into the street by Municipal policemen Wood had stationed at City Hall. Walling, soon joined by fifty Metropolitan officers, attempted to go back in but was badly outnumbered. The Board of Commissioners called out the National Guard, and the Seventh Regiment surrounded City Hall. Wood surrendered and was charged with inciting a riot. He was soon released on bail and returned to his office.

The feud continued throughout the summer of 1857. Disorder spread throughout the city as gangs turned on one another in turf wars. National Guard units were brought in to restore order. Everyone was waiting for a court decision to end the chaos. Early in the fall the courts finally handed down a decisive verdict against the Municipal police. Mayor Wood surrendered and the Municipals were disbanded. The legal status of the Metropolitan Board of Commissioners was affirmed and they began the long process of building an agency and restoring public trust. They began by adopting a new white metal badge that unified all departments in the system.

The American Civil War began in 1861 and by 1863 the federal government passed the Conscription Act, which empowered a bureau to draft those who had not volunteered for the war (see sidebar) in order to provide soldiers for its army. Draft offices opened in July and were unwelcome in New York City. Fourth of July political speeches raised public feeling against the draft as broiling summer temperatures lowered people's patience. Saturday, July 11, was the day chosen to begin the draft in the city. People talked of nothing else all weekend and the growing discontent was serious enough that Captain George Walling spent Sunday night at his station house. The still relatively new police force would soon be forced to protect the city's citizens from social unrest.

By early Monday morning on July 13 a draft riot had begun. Laborers gathered in the streets. Instead of going to their

A city in crisis
The Conscription Act

The U.S. Congress passed the Conscription Act in March of 1863. The Civil War had been going on for almost two years with no end in sight. The Union Army lacked new recruits to join the fight but also needed to control the vast number of deserters who were leaving the battlefields illegally. The new law, called the "Act for Enrolling and Calling Out the National Forces," created a national Provost Marshal Bureau. The bureau was empowered to draft those who had not volunteered, and to keep them in the army once they were enlisted under threat of criminal penalties.

Government agents conducted a census of all able-bodied, male citizens of the United States and set up a lottery in each congressional district. The new soldiers were drawn from this pool of men but there were still several ways to avoid military service. Drafted men could pay three hundred dollars, or they could provide an "acceptable

jobs they worked their way up Eighth and Ninth Avenues, closing shops and factories along the way. Other workmen joined the procession. They headed toward Central Park on the march downtown toward the ninth district provost marshal's office. The office was where the draft lottery was to be held at ten-thirty that morning.

Along the way the crowds tore down telegraph poles and lines to disrupt communication. Others used crowbars to pull up railroad tracks in an attempt to isolate the city. Rioters caught the superintendent of police, John A. Kennedy, out alone on the street. They attacked him and delivered him nearly dead to police headquarters.

Thousands of people arrived at the district office, many carrying signs saying "No Draft." The lottery began but before it could be completed the mob rushed the building and destroyed its contents, setting fire to the remains. By this time the crowds on the Upper East Side numbered over twelve thousand. Men, women, and children of every social class had shut down work in order to participate or simply watch the disturbance and see what would happen. The rioters had virtually halted all business in the city and were targeting government representatives, especially the police.

substitute," if someone else would take their place.

The new law met with a great deal of opposition in New York City. To begin with, the federal government's involvement in state and local politics was not welcomed by many New Yorkers. The exemption fee seemed to favor the wealthy while leaving the poor to do battle. Most harmful in the end was the way the law escalated racial tensions in the city. New York was a Northern city with longstanding commercial ties to Southern slavery, leaving it very sensitive to racial issues.

New York City was the national press capital for both the abolitionist (those who opposed slavery) and anti-abolitionist causes. In 1863 only whites were considered citizens of the United States and susceptible to the draft. The tension between blacks and whites grew dangerous when poor, lower-class whites felt the federal government was giving privileges to blacks while they themselves were called to risk life and livelihood in the war effort. By mid-July, New York City itself would be a battleground.

Policing a riot and earning respect

The Metropolitan police district was without a superintendent and communication lines had been cut off throughout the city. Authorities began mobilizing larger units of several hundred police to control troubled areas. By mid-afternoon the rioters had divided into those who had gathered for antidraft protesting and those who were inclined to looting, arson, and murder. After Monday the crowds turned increasingly violent toward the black community. Some associated blacks with slavery and slavery to the war, somehow making blacks responsible for the draft and the easiest target to lash out at. Blacks bore the brunt of much of the bloody violence.

With the police rising to the occasion, Walling and his patrols protected factories used for the manufacture or storage of weapons. They dispersed gangs of looters and cleared barricades off of city streets in preparation for the anticipated arrival of military help. On Wednesday, Union troops were transported to the city to restore order. The combination of troops and police collapsed the rebellion and the riots were over. Troops remained in the city for several weeks but only pockets of resistance remained.

Illustration of the 1863 draft riots in New York City. *(© Bettmann/Corbis)*

Walling was regarded as one of the heroes of the West Side forces for his part in the draft riots. He was elevated to the rank of police inspector, and eight years later he drew on his former experiences to contain a labor strike in 1871. The strike showed many of the same elements of the laborers' uprising of 1863, but it lacked the brutal racial assaults of the draft riots. Violence threatened again the following year and it was only the appearance of Inspector Walling that prevented a physical confrontation between the two sides of the strike.

On July 23, 1874, Walling was named chief of police for New York City. His wife, Sarah Bennett Walling, died several months later on November 25. Walling remained in his position as police chief until June 9, 1885. Walling held a dim view of politicians and included these reflections in his 1887 memoirs. He promoted removal of political control from the police. Since formation of the department earlier in the century, patrolmen were generally appointed through political influence.

Walling argued that the failings of the police department could be traced to the democratic process (public election of public officials) where the vote and the dollar kept a cop from honest performance of his duty. Walling died in 1891 and was buried at the family burial ground, known as Miller Avenue Cemetery in New Jersey.

For More Information

Books

Astor, Gerald. *The New York Cops: An Informal History*. New York: Charles Scribner's Sons, 1971.

Bernstein, Iver. *The New York City Draft Riots: Their Significance for American Society and Politics in the Age of the Civil War*. New York: Oxford University Press, 1990.

McCague, James. *The Second Rebellion: The Story of the New York City Draft Riots of 1863*. New York: Dial Press, Inc., 1968.

Walling, George W. *Recollections of a New York City Chief of Police*. New York: Caxton Book Concern Limited, 1887.

Where to Learn More

Books

Abadinsky, Howard. *Drug Abuse: An Introduction*. Chicago, IL: Nelson-Hall Publishers, 1997.

Acker, James R., Robert M. Bohm, and Charles S. Lanier, eds. *America's Experiment with Capital Punishment: Reflections on the Past, Present, and Future of the Ultimate Penal Sanction*. Durham, NC: Carolina Academic Press, 1998.

Anderson, Elijah. *Streetwise: Race, Class and Change in an Urban Community*. Chicago, IL: University of Chicago Press, 1990.

Arrigo, Bruce A., ed. *Social Justice, Criminal Justice*. Belmont, CA: Wadsworth, 1999.

Austern, David. *The Crime Victims Handbook: Your Rights and Role in the Criminal Justice System*. New York: Viking, 1987.

Bachman-Prehn, Ronet D. *Death and Violence on the Reservation: Homicide, Violence, and Suicide in American Indian Populations*. New York: Auburn House, 1992.

Baum, Lawrence. *American Courts*. 5th ed. Boston: Houghton Mifflin, 2001.

Belknap, Joanne. *The Invisible Woman: Gender, Crime, and Justice*. Toronto: Wadsworth Thomson Learning, 2001.

Benjamin, William P. *African Americans in the Criminal Justice System*. New York: Vantage Press, 1996.

Besharov, Douglas J. *Recognizing Child Abuse: A Guide for the Concerned*. New York: Free Press, 1990.

Burns, Ronald G., and Michael J. Lynch. *Environmental Crime: A Source Book*. New York: LFB Scholarly Publishing, 2004.

Burrough, Bryan. *Public Enemies: America's Greatest Crime Wave and the Birth of the FBI, 1933–34*. New York: Penguin Press, 2004.

Buzawa, Eve, and Carl Buzawa. *Domestic Violence: The Criminal Justice Response*. Thousand Oaks, CA: Sage, 1996.

Carp, Robert A., and Ronald Stidham. *Judicial Process in America*. 5th ed. Washington, DC: CQ Press, 2001.

Chase, Anthony. *Law and History: The Evolution of the American Legal System*. New York: The New Press, 1997.

Clement, Mary. *The Juvenile Justice System*. 3rd ed. Woburn, MA: Butterworth Heinemann, 2002.

Clifford, Mary. *Environmental Crime: Enforcement, Policy, and Social Responsibility*. Gaithersburg, MD: Aspen Publishers, Inc., 1998.

Clifford, Ralph D., ed. *Cybercrime: The Investigation, Prosecution, and Defense of a Computer-Related Crime*. Durham, NC: Carolina Academic Press, 2001.

Cohn, Marjorie, and David Dow. *Cameras in the Courtroom: Television and the Pursuit of Justice*. New York: McFarland & Company, 1998.

Coloroso, Barbara. *The Bully, the Bullied, and the Bystander: From Pre-School to High School, How Parents and Teachers Can Help Break the Cycle of Violence*. New York: HarperResource, 2003.

Conser, James A., and Gregory D. Russell. *Law Enforcement in the United States*. Gaithersburg, MD: Aspen, 2000.

Cromwell, Paul, Lee Parker, and Shawna Mobley. "The Five-Finger Discount." In *In Their Own Words: Criminals on Crime*, edited by Paul Cromwell. Los Angeles, CA: Roxbury, pp. 57–70.

Curran, Daniel J., and Claire M. Renzetti. *Theories of Crime*. Boston: Allyn & Bacon, 2001.

Davidson, Michael J. *A Guide to Military Criminal Law*. Annapolis, MD: Naval Institute Press, 1999.

Dummer, Harry R. *Religion in Corrections*. Lanham, MD: American Correctional Associates, 2000.

Dunne, Dominick. *Justice: Crimes, Trials, and Punishment*. New York: Three Rivers Press, 2002.

Federal Bureau of Investigation. *Crime in the United States, 2002: Uniform Crime Reports*. Washington, DC: U.S. Department of Justice, 2003.

Felson, Marcus. *Crime and Everyday Life.* 2nd ed. Thousand Oaks, CA: Pine Forge Press, 1998.

Frank, Nancy, and Michael Lynch. *Corporate Crime, Corporate Violence.* Albany, NY: Harrow and Heston, 1992.

Friedman, Lawrence M. *Crime and Punishment in American History.* New York: Basic Books, 1993.

Garbarino, James. *Lost Boys: Why Our Sons Turn Violent and How We Can Save Them.* New York: Free Press, 1999.

Gordon, Margaret, and Stephanie Riger. *The Female Fear.* New York: Free Press, 1989.

Hirsch, Adam Jay. *The Rise of the Penitentiary: Prisons and Punishment in Early America.* New Haven, CT: Yale University Press, 1992.

Hoffer, Peter C. *Law and People in Colonial America.* Baltimore: Johns Hopkins University Press, 1998.

Jones-Brown, Delores. *Race, Crime, and Punishment.* Philadelphia: Chelsea House, 2000.

Karmen, Andrew. *Crime Victims: An Introduction to Victimology.* 4th ed. Belmont, CA: Wadsworth, 2001.

Lane, Brian. *Crime and Detection.* New York: Alfred A. Knopf, 1998.

Levin, Jack. *The Violence of Hate: Confronting Racism, Anti-Semitism, and Other Forms of Bigotry.* Boston: Allyn and Bacon, 2002.

Lunde, Paul. *Organized Crime: An Inside Guide to the World's Most Successful Industry.* New York: DK Publishing, Inc., 2004.

Lyman, Michael D., and Gary W. Potter. *Organized Crime.* Upper Saddle River, NJ: Pearson Prentice Hall, 2004.

Mones, Paul. *When a Child Kills.* New York: Simon & Schuster, 1991.

Oliver, Willard M. *Community-Oriented Policing: A Systematic Approach to Policing.* Upper Saddle River, NJ: Prentice Hall, 2001.

Patrick, John J. *The Young Oxford Companion to the Supreme Court of the United States.* New York: Oxford University Press, 1998.

Ramsey, Sarah H., and Douglas E. Adams. *Children and the Law in a Nutshell.* 2nd ed. St. Paul, MN: Thomson/West, 2003.

Renzetti, Claire M., and Lynne Goodstein, eds. *Women, Crime, and Criminal Justice.* Los Angeles: Roxbury, 2001.

Russell, Katheryn. *The Color of Crime.* New York: New York University Press, 1998.

Sherman, Mark. *Introduction to Cyber Crime.* Washington, DC: Federal Judicial Center, 2000.

Siegel, Larry J. *Criminology: The Core.* Belmont, CA: Wadsworth/Thomson Learning, 2002.

Silverman, Ira. *Corrections: A Comprehensive View.* 2nd ed. Belmont, CA: Wadsworth, 2001.

Situ, Yingyi, and David Emmons. *Environmental Crime: The Criminal Justice System's Role in Protecting the Environment.* Thousand Oaks, CA: Sage Publications, 2000.

Smith, Helen. *The Scarred Heart: Understanding and Identifying Kids Who Kill.* Knoxville, TN: Callisto, 2000.

Stark, Rodney, and Williams Sims Bainbridge. *Religion, Deviance, and Social Control.* New York: Routledge, 1997.

Sullivan, Robert, ed. *Mobsters and Gangsters: Organized Crime in America, from Al Capone to Tony Soprano.* New York: Life Books, 2002.

Sutherland, Edwin H. *White-Collar Crime: The Uncut Version.* New Haven, CT: Yale University Press, 1983.

Walker, Samuel. *The Police in America: An Introduction.* New York: McGraw-Hill, 1992.

Wilkinson, Charles F. *American Indians, Time, and the Law: Native Societies in a Modern Constitutional Democracy.* New Haven, CN: Yale University Press, 1987.

Wright, Richard, and Scott Decker. *Armed Robbers in Action: Stickups and Street Culture.* Boston: Northeastern University Press, 1997.

Yalof, David A., and Kenneth Dautrich. *The First Amendment and the Media in the Court of Public Opinion.* Cambridge: Cambridge University Press, 2002.

Web Sites

"Arrest the Racism: Racial Profiling in America." *American Civil Liberties Union (ACLU).* http://www.aclu.org/profiling (accessed on September 20, 2004).

Center for the Prevention of School Violence. http://www.ncdjjdp.org/cpsv/ (accessed on September 20, 2004).

"Computer Crime and Intellectual Property Section (CCIPS) of the Criminal Division." *U.S. Department of Justice.* http://www.cybercrime.gov (accessed on September 20, 2004).

"Counterfeit Division." *United States Secret Service.* http://www.secretservice.gov/counterfeit.shtml (accessed on September 20, 2004).

Court TV's Crime Library. http://www.crimelibrary.com (accessed on September 20, 2004).

"Criminal Enforcement." *U.S. Environmental Protection Agency.* http://www.epa.gov/compliance/criminal/index.html (accessed on September 20, 2004).

Death Penalty Information Center. http://www.deathpenaltyinfo.org (accessed on September 20, 2004).

Department of Homeland Security. http://www.dhs.gov (accessed on September 20, 2004).

Federal Bureau of Investigation (FBI). http://www.fbi.gov (accessed on September 20, 2004).

McGeary, Johanna. "Who's the Enemy Now?" *Time,* March 29, 2004. http://www.time.com/time/classroom/glenfall2004/pg28.html (accessed on September 20, 2004).

Mothers Against Drunk Driving (MADD). http://www.madd.org (accessed on September 20, 2004).

National Alliance of Crime Investigators Associations. http://www.nagia.org (accessed on September 20, 2004).

National Center for Juvenile Justice. http://www.ncjj.org (accessed on September 20, 2004).

National Center for Victims of Crime. http://www.ncvc.org (accessed on September 20, 2004).

National Child Abuse and Neglect Data System (NCANDS). http://nccanch. acf.hhs.gov/index.cfm (accessed on September 20, 2004).

"National Institute of Corrections (NIC)." *U.S. Department of Justice.* http://www.nicic.org (accessed on September 20, 2004).

National Institute of Military Justice. http://www.nimj.com/Home.asp (accessed on September 20, 2004).

National Organization for Victim Assistance (NOVA). http://www.try-nova. org (accessed on September 20, 2004).

Uniform Crime Reporting Program. http://www.fbi.gov/ucr/ucr.htm (accessed on September 20, 2004).

United Nations Office for Drug Control and Crime Prevention, Organized Crime. http://www.undcp.org/organized_crime.html (accessed on September 20, 2004).

U.S. Courts. http://www.uscourts.gov (accessed on September 20, 2004).

U.S. Department of Justice. http://www.usdoj.gov (accessed on September 20, 2004).

U.S. Drug Enforcement Administration. http://www.dea.gov (accessed on September 20, 2004).

U.S. Securities and Exchange Commission. http://www.sec.gov (accessed on September 20, 2004).

Index

Boldface indicates main entries and their page numbers; illustrations are marked by (ill.)